Instructor's Manual

CASES AND POLICIES IN
PERSONNEL/HUMAN RESOURCES MANAGEMENT

Fifth Edition

Raymond L. Hilgert
Sterling H. Schoen
Joseph W. Towle
School of Business and Public Administration
Washington University

HOUGHTON MIFFLIN COMPANY   BOSTON

Dallas   Geneva, Illinois
Lawrenceville, New Jersey   Palo Alto

Printed in the U.S.A.

ISBN: 0-395-40419-3

ABCDEFGHIJ-A-898765

CONTENTS

iii

CONTENTS

CONTENTS

v

This <u>Instructor's Manual</u> is designed to assist the instructor who uses the materials in the fifth edition of <u>Cases and Policies in Personnel/Human Resources Management</u>, either in the college classroom or in a management training program. The manual reflects, of course, main features of the text: its functional parts; its pretested cases; its emphasis on behavioral applications of personnel/human resources management, on equal opportunity employment, and on other contemporary issues that influence employer-employee relationships.

Instructors who are familiar with the book will note that we have retained the same title from the previous edition. We believe that the term "personnel/human resources management" adequately encompasses the scope of the cases and policies included in the text. Managers and supervisors in every organization spend most of their time working with and through people--their human resources. The cases and policies presented in the text emphasize this facet of organizational life and the importance of effective personnel/human resources management, organizational understanding, and supervisory skills.

The text is adaptable for use in courses or seminars in personnel management, human resources management, organizational behavior, organization and administration, supervision, and the like. The classification of cases by parts should help the instructor who is looking for a case study to illustrate a particular concept or issue. In this <u>Instructor's Manual</u>, we have included case method analyses, techniques, and experiences--either our own or the case contributor's. We have done so only for the instructor's consideration; every instructor's own personal analysis and decisions will determine his or her approach to the study of a case. For most cases, we have included questions and suggestions. "Suggestions" seems to us more appropriate than "answers," since there usually is no one answer to any personnel/human resources management problem.

In considering each case, the instructor may want to ask these general background questions: (1) What are the problems in the case? (2) What facts are relevant to these problems? (3) What are the alternative solutions to the problems? and (4) Which solution should be selected and implemented and why?

The success of any case discussion depends primarily on the skill and ingenuity of the discussion leader. We hope that this Instructor's Manual will, in fact, assist the instructor in directing that skill and ingenuity to successful and meaningful learning experiences.

R.L.H.
S.H.S.
J.W.T.

THE CASE STUDY METHOD IN MANAGEMENT EDUCATION AND TRAINING

The case method of education and training is a widely accepted technique for the teaching of management in the United States. In addition, universities, private companies, and government agencies in England, France, Germany, Italy, Switzerland, Korea, Japan, and other countries have experimented with and adopted the case method of management instruction. Instructors using case studies in either schools or departments of administration, or in management development programs sponsored by universities or companies, should have a clear understanding of the case method and its application.

WHAT IS A CASE?

A case is a written record of a specific situation that has actually confronted individuals. A case may include not only the facts of the situation, but also the feelings, opinions, and prejudices that the individuals involved in the situation may have experienced and that may have influenced their actions. In studying a case, students do not read and discuss general theories. Rather, they study specific facts, feelings, and opinions from which decisions must be made. This requires the study of a realistic situation, analysis of it, and arrival at logical decisions.

WHAT IS THE CASE METHOD?

The case method of teaching possesses two distinguishing features. The first of these stems from the materials with which the student works. The student is required to work not with theoretical materials, but with actual situations. Analyses and conclusions are concerned not with "ultimate truths," but with the specific situation under consideration.

People who are not familiar with the case method often find it difficult to understand that cases are not designed primarily as examples or illustrations of "principles" or "rules." Rather, cases basically serve as a means for teaching students to think in the presence of new situations. Malcolm McNair, an advocate of the case method, described the case method as:

> class discussion of possibilities, probabilities,
> expedients--the possibilities of the combinations
> of very intricate facts, the probabilities of
> human reactions, and the expedients most likely

to bring about the responses in others that lead
to a definite end.[1]

The second distinguishing feature relates to the environment
in which the learning experience takes place. Classroom and conference activity is student-centered. The instructor should make
it clear to students that they are responsible for working through
the case problems. The student must participate and become involved in both the teaching and learning processes. Each student
has the opportunity to teach other students both inside and outside
the classroom. A free and frequent exchange of ideas among class
or conference members constitutes one of the important requirements for using the case method. Equally important, the instructor
should not assume the role of an expert who knows more about the
case than the participants in the discussion do. The instructor
should create a democratic environment that permits the students
to freely express their ideas, and in which they are stimulated
to think and to rely upon their own conclusions. The students must
find the problem or problems in the case; they must engage in the
analysis; they must consider alternative solutions; they must select the best alternative available under the circumstances; and
they must provide for putting the solution into effect.

THE OBJECTIVE OF THE CASE METHOD

The basic objective of the case method is to develop management skills in administration, which essentially means making
and carrying out decisions that enable a business organization to
achieve its objectives.[2] Any manager must carry out decisions
through the efforts of other people, which means motivating people
to work toward the goals of the organization.

Administrative skills are acquired most effectively by a person's doing, rather than hearing, observing, or reading about what
another has learned. No one can become a professional baseball
player by reading about the game or by listening to lectures on
the subject. To learn the game, baseball players must get on the
field and actually throw, catch, bat, and run. They must practice
these skills before they become proficient. Similarly, the development of administrative skills requires that skills be developed
in the process of practice.

---

1. Malcolm P. McNair, ed., The Case Method at the Harvard
Business School (New York: McGraw-Hill, 1954), p. 4.

2. Administration is defined here as the ability: (1) to
assign to each decision that needs to be rendered its proper priority and effort; (2) to make or have made intelligent decisions on
the issue at hand; and (3) to get decisions carried out effectively
once they have been made, in order to promote the objectives of the
organization in the most efficient manner consistent with the cultural values and public policy of the society in which it exists.

Education for management leadership embraces objectives very similar to those in the teaching of other professions such as law, medicine, and engineering. The common objective of schools that teach all of these professions is to find ways of solving selected problems by developing useful ways of thinking and acting. They all rely upon class discussion as one of their principal techniques for teaching. The instructor asks questions and listens; students talk, analyze, and decide upon situations. They pit their analyses and decisions against those of their classmates. Their principal tools consist of cases that they analyze and diagnose in class-rooms, laboratories, and clinics. The end objective is to develop doctors, lawyers, engineers, and managers who are prepared to accept responsibility for actions and decisions involving other people.[3]

ROLE OF THE INSTRUCTOR

Successful use of the case method of teaching assumes that a democratic relationship exists between instructor and student. This does not mean that the instructor serves no useful function; nor does it mean that the instructor need not be a scholar or competent in the field of management studies. However, the instructor using the case method is called upon to utilize teaching skills to a greater degree than to use scholarly knowledge.

The case method requires that discussions get somewhere. The instructor must be a good listener in order to interpret not only the students' words, but also their feelings and attitudes. The instructor must be prepared to help them to progress toward their goal by: (1) asking questions--the right kinds of questions, (2) helping them to express their ideas--but not distorting those ideas, and (3) voicing opinions and drawing upon knowledge appropriate to the situation.

The instructor's questions should not be designed to steer the students on a predetermined course, nor should they be designed to test or to embarrass students. Questions should be used to initiate and promote discussion and to help students progress along paths they have found for themselves. The instructor can also assist the students by periodically summarizing progress that has been made and by restating ideas that have been imperfectly or incompletely expressed.

The instructor's own opinions should be voiced with care. If the instructor states views or positions before students have concluded their analysis, this may shut off discussion for students who disagree and may overly encourage those students who agree. If the instructor recites at length from personal experiences and knowledge, this may silence those students who cannot muster the weight of such authority. The instructor's own sentiments and

---

3. Kenneth R. Andrews, ed., The Case Method of Teaching Human Relations and Administration (Cambridge, Mass.: Harvard University Press, 1953), p. 39.

conclusions, if injected at an early stage in the case analysis, may change his or her role from that of a participant to that of an authoritarian outsider.

However, after the students have concluded their analysis, the instructor may express opinions and conclusions concerning the case, provided this is not done with the intent or effect of telling students that the instructor's analysis is the correct one and that theirs is incorrect. The instructor must not create in students' minds the feeling that judgment is being passed upon their work.

The class or conference cannot be expected to deal with all problems that arise without occasionally providing technical information. Short lectures may precede or conclude a case discussion, or may interrupt it if students find this necessary in order to obtain technical knowledge necessary for continuing the discussion.

ADVANTAGES AND LIMITATIONS OF THE CASE METHOD

The case method possesses many favorable attributes that should be recognized.

1. The cases are interesting. They are about people—their successes and failures. They are about specific situations in real life.

2. Cases provide experiences that enable students to learn the skills a manager needs in order to be successful at supervising others. The students acquire practice in making managerial decisions and carrying them out in a manner that will obtain the support and approval of the other people in the organization.

3. The case method stimulates students to think analytically and constructively in an organizational context. This occurs, first, because each student's analyses and decisions are critically evaluated by classmates. Cases require students to justify their solutions—and, if unable to do so, to endure the disapproval of other students. Second, students must place themselves in the role of the manager and develop solutions that would be useful in the particular situation at hand.

4. The case method stimulates the development of attitudes of inquiry, questioning, and analysis. The student learns that each new situation requires fresh analysis and fresh solutions. In this process there is a translation of textbook knowledge to its application in real problems.

While the case method has proved to be very useful in management education and training, it does possess limitations:

1. The case method is more useful in teaching managerial skills than it is in supplying the technical information often required

to analyze the case and make an effective decision. For example, much of the technical information involved in wage and salary administration or collective bargaining cannot be efficiently taught by means of the case method.

2. The case method assumes that the student possesses at least a basic amount of technical knowledge in certain aspects of a business or other type of organization. It assumes that the student possesses maturity. The student must possess a sense of responsibility required to make "reasonable" decisions.

3. The case is but a part of the total situation. It may not contain all the facts, feelings, and technical data that existed in the real situation. In other words, it may be oversimplified. This oversimplification arises out of the case writer's need to limit the scope of the situation in the economy of time. It also arises out of the fact that the case writer must select the relevant facts and feelings of the situation. Neither of these simplifications occur in real life.

4. A case often cannot carry out the entire problem-solving and decision-making process. For example, very few cases enable the student to follow up on the effectiveness of a decision made in the classroom or seminar setting.

SUMMARY

The case method has proved a success in the United States in large measure because it is consistent with the American culture. The case method reflects the democratic type of teacher-student, parent-child, and boss-worker relationship that is developing in the United States. For example, it enables the college teacher to become closely involved with students in the classroom without losing status. In the final analysis, the teacher's status with students rests upon scholarly knowledge, an ability to teach, and interest in students as individual people. The instructor requires few outward signs of status to maintain this "position."

There is no one case method. It is not a static concept. Different cases have been developed to serve different purposes in business. Each instructor must adapt the case method to his or her own personality and needs. No two instructors will conduct a case discussion in exactly the same manner, just as no two teachers will give the same lecture.

In summary, the case is based upon (1) the use of real-life situations and (2) a reliance upon the creative, analytical, and decision-making powers of the student. It changes the instructor's role from that of a dispenser of knowledge to that of democratic leader of a group of which he or she becomes an integral, important part.

SMALL GROUP CASE STUDY

The philosophy and purposes of the case study method have been described, and it is recognized that students' participation and personal involvement in the case have educational and developmental value. When classes or discussion groups are large, participation by all group members is difficult. Free expression and exchange of ideas by all in the group are almost impossible. The small group case study discussion technique is a practical approach to this problem.

In brief, the small group or "buzz session" approach requires that the membership of a large group be divided into small groups for purposes of discussion of case problems or questions presented by the instructor. Usually the groups are made up of six to ten individuals. The first order of business for the group is to select a chairperson and possibly a secretary to record major points discussed. After a period of analysis and discussion of the problem or the case assignment, all groups reassemble in a plenary session. The chairperson of each small group presents a summary of the findings, conclusions, and recommendations of each group's discussion. The length of time allotted by the instructor for small group discussion depends upon the situation. A small problem or question might be discussed in a few minutes, while a case discussion might require an hour or more.

There are numerous variations of the small group or "buzz session" method. For many years the Commonwealth Edison Company conducted luncheon meetings for large groups of managers. The participants sat at luncheon tables in groups of eight or ten people. Frequently, those at each table were asked to discuss a company problem or question for a short period after lunch, and, subsequently, each table chairperson gave to the entire group the ideas, suggestions, or conclusions of those who participated in the table discussion.

A popular usage of the group discussion technique is known as "Phillips 66." It was developed by Dr. J. Donald Phillips of Hillsdale College. This approach is most useful in achieving participation by members of a large group in the analysis of a problem. It requires the division of the large group into small groups of six members each, and these groups discuss the question for six minutes. Reports from group leaders are usually called for, and the results frequently are a source of new ideas--creative thinking.

Obviously, most case studies such as those in this text require considerably more than six minutes of small group discussion. The advantages of dividing large groups into small units for discussion purposes are manifold. All members of a class or conference can participate and contribute their thinking to the analysis. This pooled judgment and occasional creative thinking have great value. Also, a more thorough analysis of a case or topic can be made, because several approaches to the problems are contributed simultaneously by the several groups. Certainly, the greater participation by members of the group elicits numerous benefits, but one of the greatest advantages of small group discussions is the enthusiasm and interest developed among group members because the activity is enjoyable. They like it.

For a more detailed discussion of the small group case study approach as experienced by instructors at Washington University, see Sterling H. Schoen and Raymond L. Hilgert, "Small Group Case Study," Improving College and University Teaching 12, No. 1 (Winter 1964): 31-35.

ROLE PLAY AND ARBITRATION CASE SIMULATION

Another useful technique that can be implemented as part of the case method of teaching is role play. At some point in a case discussion, the instructor assigns a number of students to act out certain assigned roles of the principal characters in a case for the benefit of the entire group.

The instructor may wish to structure a role play along certain preconceived lines. He or she will instruct the participating students as to the general type of role they should assume. (An example of this type of structuring is provided in this manual for the Olympic Corporation case.) Or, an instructor may prefer simply to assign case roles to the students, leaving it to the students' judgment as to how to interpret and play the roles. A number of the cases in the text are especially adaptable to role-playing situations; several in this manual have been supplied with suggestions as to problem approaches for the role plays.

Role playing is particularly valuable to the student participants because it forces them to become personally involved in developing solutions to problem situations. Students often become emotionally involved in the roles they play. At the conclusion of a role play, the instructor usually asks the group to criticize the performance, and it is usually apparent that human feelings and emotions have colored the behavior exhibited.

Arbitration Case Simulation is a somewhat specialized form of role play that is appropriate for certain cases involving labor unions. Several of the cases, particularly in Part Seven, are ideally suited for arbitration case simulation. As practiced at Washington University, the approach is as follows:

1. Witnesses for each side--management and union--are required to prepare and submit to the chief arbitrator (the instructor) a trial brief of their case as they would present it to the arbitration board (the other class members). This trial brief is to include: (a) a listing or outline of the relevant, important facts, with a brief statement of evidence intended to prove those facts; and (b) an outline of the legal argument to be made, with quotations from the contract, statutes, or arbitrators in similar cases.

2. The witnesses for the union and management present their cases to the chief arbitrator and the arbitration board in the following order:
    a. Union--not to exceed 5 minutes
    b. Management--not to exceed 5 minutes

    c. Union rebuttal and additional arguments--not to exceed 3 minutes

    d. Management rebuttal and additional arguments--not to exceed 3 minutes

3. Following initial presentations and rebuttal, the class arbitration board is given the opportunity to cross-examine the witnesses. Members of the arbitration board may direct questions to any management or union witnesses as they request.

4. The arbitration board votes upon a ruling in the case. (The chief arbitrator, of course, is not allowed to vote.)

    Following the class vote, the instructor may wish to read to the class excerpts from the actual decision of the arbitrator, if this is available. This is done for the purpose of comparing the class decision with that of the arbitrator. If the class decision differs from that of the arbitrator, this can provide a fruitful area for further discussion in order to compare the type of decision reasoning that entered into both the students' and arbitrator's decisions.[1]

---

    1. For a further discussion of this approach, see Raymond L. Hilgert, "Arbitration Case Simulation: A Classroom Experience," The Journal of Business Education (January 1965).

WRITTEN CASES

At times the instructor may wish to use a case as a written exercise. The grading of a written case should be based primarily upon a student's logical analysis and development of the case and his or her solution, not upon the decision that a student chooses in and of itself.

As a guide for grading written case papers, the authors have developed and used a number of grading "check sheets" for courses at Washington University. One such grading sheet has been used for a one-semester graduate course in "Personnel Management Analysis" and is reproduced below. During this one-semester course, the graduate students are required to submit several cases in written form, and the grading of these cases is based largely upon the degree to which the student's efforts meet the criteria of the grading sheet. The written cases are returned to the students accompanied by the grading sheet with instructor's comments.

Another approach to written case evaluation included in this manual has been provided by John R. Hundley III, who has taught undergraduate personnel management courses in Washington University's University College Division. This "check-list" approach, also reproduced below, may be preferred by some instructors, since it can be quickly scored by the person evaluating the written case.

PERSONNEL MANAGEMENT CASE EVALUATION[1]

I. Organization and Presentation of the Report

A. The organization of your report was:

____Interesting and effective;____Adequate;____Difficult to follow

B. Your spelling and grammar were:

____Effective and correct;____Adequate;____Often incorrect

C. Your writing style was:

____Interesting and effective;____Adequate;____Lacking in quality

____Vocabulary and sentence structure of high quality

----

1. Prepared by Dr. Raymond L. Hilgert, Graduate School of Business Administration, Washington University.

_____Sentence structure weak

_____Sentences short and choppy

_____Incomplete sentences

D. Comments_____

_____

_____

_____

II. Subject Matter Development

A. Your statement of case problem(s) was:

_____Clear and concise;_____Adequate;_____Superficial or vague

B. Your recognition of the most important factor(s) was:

_____Complete;_____Good;_____Adequate;_____Poor;_____Unsatisfactory

C. Your coverage of the important factor(s) and considerations was:

_____Complete;_____Good;_____Adequate;_____Poor;_____Inadequate

_____All points were covered in a balanced way

_____Most points covered in a balanced way

_____Serious gaps in coverage

_____Little or no balance

_____Spent too much time on minor details

D. Comments_____

_____

_____

_____

III. Conclusions and Recommendations

A. The factual basis of your conclusions and recommendations was:

_____Very discriminating;_____Good;_____Adequate;_____Poor;_____

_____Inadequate

11

____You did (not) examine the character of the data, distinguish-
ing among facts, opinions, and your own inferences

____You did (not) identify enough facts to provide a sound basis

____Your understanding of case facts was not always in accord
with the statements of the case

____You made suggestions without first considering their feasi-
bility or such things as availability, time, and cost

____Too much rehash of case facts

B. Your conclusions and recommendations were:

____Very thorough;____Good;____Acceptable;____Questionable

____Inappropriate

____You did (not) provide for carrying out your decision(s)

____You did (not) examine problems that might be created

____You explored the possibility of alternatives that are not in
the case

____You failed to reach a definite decision that left no doubt
as to where you stood

____Your decision was conditional and you did not state the alter-
native

C. Comments_____

_____

_____

_____

WRITTEN CASE EVALUATION FORM[2]

	EVALUATION		
	excellent	average	poor

I. Organization and Presentation of Report

1. Report legible and on 8 1/2 x 11" sheets _____

2. Report between 3 and 5 pages long _____

3. Organization of report easy to follow _____

4. Spelling and grammar correct _____

5. Writing style interesting and effective _____

II. Contents of Report

A. Problem Definition

1. Case problem(s) correctly identified _____

2. Statement of problem(s) was clear and concise _____

3. Immediate and long-range problems considered _____

B. Analysis

1. Distinguished between symptoms and causes _____

2. Distinguished between fact, opinion, and own inferences _____

3. All important factors recognized _____

4. Avoided excessive rehash of case facts _____

5. Reflected good understanding of text material _____

----

2. Prepared by John R. Hundley III, Instructor in the University College Division of Washington University.

	excellent	average	poor

C. Solutions

    1. All feasible solutions identi-
       fied

    2. Solutions consistent with defi-
       nition of problem

    3. Each solution evaluated in
       terms of risk, cost, timing,
       etc.

D. Recommendations

    1. You left no doubt as to which
       solution you recommended

    2. The solution that you selected
       followed logically from your
       analysis and evaluation

    3. You provided for the imple-
       mentation of your decision(s)

E. Maintained proper balance among
    problem definition, analysis,
    solutions, and recommendations

                FINAL EVALUATION

ORGANIZATIONAL ANALYSIS

The authors have found that in addition to the case materials presented in this text, it is often desirable to have students do a "real-world analysis" of a business institution or nonprofit enterprise, or of a unit of a larger organization. At the graduate level of human resources management study, we have had students undertake projects involving an in-depth study and analysis of an organization with which they are familiar or one where they can get access to information. This typically requires the students to visit the organization; to talk with managers, supervisors, and employees; and to study documents and publications of the organization that are made available to them. Each student is required to submit a report discussing the type, size, and regular functions of the enterprise, including the student's conclusions regarding the organization's objectives, policies, structures, operations, and so forth.

The following is a list of survey-type questions that can be provided to the students to assist them in doing their organizational analysis. It should be noted that these questions could be adapted to any number of the case materials in this text, since they are basic organizational and human resources management questions.

SURVEY QUESTIONS FOR ORGANIZATIONAL ANALYSIS

1. Purpose or objectives:
   a. Are the objectives of the enterprise clearly stated and understandable?
   b. Are the objectives realistic, attainable, and verifiable?
   c. Are the objectives of the organization communicated in writing or verbally? If the latter, do all key personnel perceive and understand these purposes? Are they committed to them?
   d. How are major objectives established?
   e. How are minor (departmental or unit) objectives established?

2. Policies:
   a. Are there written policies that are used as guidelines for the organization?
   b. Is there agreement among key management personnel regarding the unwritten policies, and are they used in the administration of the organization?
   c. How are the objectives and policies of the organization translated into plans-of-action, systems, procedures, and operations?

    d. Are written documents such as a constitution, a charter, or written policies available for study and use by members of the organization?

3. Structure:
   a. How have responsibilities and work activities been divided at the top-management level? At the middle-management level? At the supervisory level? (Division of labor)
   b. To what extent has the principle of "specialization" been used in the "fixing of responsibilities" in the organization?
   c. On what bases (such as functions, products, activities, etc.) are operations and work activities grouped together?
   d. What is the "span of control" used at various levels in the organization? Have responsibility and authority been delegated adequately, and does each individual in a key position understand his or her "accountability for results"?
   e. How many "levels of management" are there in the organization structure--and are line communications adequate? (This structure can probably be presented best with an organization chart.)

4. Informal organization:
   a. Evaluate both the formal and informal communication systems in the organization.
   b. Are the authority and leadership of the appointed (or elected) managers accepted by subordinates? At the top-management level? At the middle-management level? At the supervisory level?
   c. Are there informal leaders in the organization who influence operations? Do these influences contribute to organizational efficiency and morale or do they tend to restrict productivity?
   d. Are there small informal groups or cliques within the larger organization, and what is their influence?

5. Personnel:
   a. Is top-management adequately performing the functions of planning, organizing, directing, and controlling the activities of the enterprise?
   b. At each managerial level (top, middle, and supervisory) are leadership and coordination adequately provided for all members of the organization?
   c. Are the personnel needs of the organization properly assessed and forecast?
   d. Are the operations of the enterprise adequately staffed? Is a productive labor force properly selected and trained?
   e. Are wage and salary plans for employees developed and administered in accordance with professional standards and procedures?
   f. Do working conditions for employees (including health and safety programs) provide the best possible environment for individuals that the work situation permits?

g. Are the attitudes and aspirations of employees recognized
    and considered in the making of management decisions? To
    what extent is "participative management" used in the oper-
    ations of the organization?

6. Problems in the organization:
    a. What are the principal organizational problems within the
        enterprise?
    b. What facts, events, and conditions are pertinent to the
        analysis of these problems?
    c. What alternatives are available to management for the solu-
        tion of these problems?

7. Conclusions and recommendations:
    a. Summary of the "key points" recognized in the survey.
    b. Recommendations to management for the continued successful
        operations of the organization and for the solution of the
        organizational problems. (Major proposals might require
        the development of a new organization structure depicted
        by a proposed organizational chart.)

PART ONE

THE PERSONNEL/HUMAN RESOURCES MANAGEMENT FUNCTION

CASE 1

PACIFIC AIRCRAFT COMPANY

This comprehensive case was selected as the first case in the text, because it aptly demonstrates the pervasive nature of the personnel/human resources management function. Some instructors may wish to use this case as an initial case to sensitize students to the many areas of organizational life where personnel/human resources management plays a role. Alternatively, instructors may prefer to use this case as a "capstone," or final summary case, after students have become more familiar with the topic areas normally included in a personnel/human resources management course of study.

The case itself describes numerous personnel problems in a company of 1,550 employees. A consultant has been hired to identify and present a plan to stem the company's problems. Various issues are described through the perspectives of the company's president and personnel staff members and from the observations the consultant is able to make on his/her initial visit through the company. The case is written to require each student to place himself/herself in the consultant's position and role.

Numerous personnel problems and issues currently exist within the company, and a partial list is outlined below. In conjunction with this list of problems are commentaries and a brief, suggested plan of action for each issue. Instructors may wish to structure the class discussion around the formulation of solutions to these and other problems identified in the case, and the suggestions below should serve to assist in guiding that discussion.

Personnel/Human Resources Problem	Commentary and Possible Plan of Action
1. Decline of company goodwill within the community.	Corporate goodwill is important to the company's position in a community, and it is an important factor in attracting a strong and loyal work force. No company operates in a vacuum, as Ms. Gregory's comments seem to indicate. Establishing minority recruitment efforts and an investigation into the Lake Winemea issue could serve several purposes: e.g., enhance the company's reputation as a responsible entity; secure

21

a more heterogeneous work force in compliance with EEOC guidelines; and eliminate/mitigate the probability of government regulation on both fronts.

2. Compliance with EEOC guide-lines.

Hire an additional personnel staff member to deal exclusively with EEOC compliance issues. The company's size justifies this expansion; more importantly, its involvement with government contracts mandates greater attention to EEOC and affirmative action regulations.

3. High incidence of turnover and absenteeism rates.

Finding replacements only treats the symptoms without identifying the causes and correcting the problems. There appears to be little effort to establish corporate accountability for these problems. Instead, they are explained away as being part of a declining "work ethic." Several aternatives might be utilized: e.g., identification of objective targets for absenteeism and turnover rates; comparison of those rates against actual results to pinpoint problem areas within the company; continual monitoring of employees' absenteeism records to spot and solve problems and prevent the need for termination; increased attention to guidance for employees having performance problems; use of exit interviews both to salvage potential quits and as a source of important information for improving management practices.

4. Understaffing of the personnel department.

To expect a personnel department staff of three persons to handle increasingly complex responsibilities in a company of more than 1,500 employees is to ask the near impossible. The situation helps explain Gregory's at-titude regarding EEOC compliance, paperwork, etc. The staff is spread too thin to ac-complish the tasks it faces. Perhaps this also accounts for the discrepancy between Gregory's work force demographics and Brace and Walker's assumptions. The circumstances may be changing so quickly that no one is kept up-to-date. Reassess the nature of the positions and responsibilities of the current personnel staff members with the needs of the company. Even though both Gregory and Brace are spending time with government regulatory material and correspondence, still the job is not getting done properly. Restructure the responsibilities to avoid redundancy in effort, while assuring that proper attention is given to the tasks. Hire additional staff members and specialize those positions as circumstances warrant.

5. Lack of documentation to support contract personnel specifications and requirements.

    In conjunction with the expansion of the personnel staff, institute a formalized and detailed system to identify and track the company's efforts to meet government specifications (another specialized position, perhaps).

6. Inadequate recruitment efforts.

    The company needs to implement a dual recruitment effort—one for white-collar employees and one for blue-collar workers who constitute 85 percent of the total work force. Each group has unique concerns that merit attention. Since it appears that Brace is making progress compiling information on the white-collar positions, particular emphasis should be given to production employees. In order to better match job applicants with available positions, job descriptions and job specifications must be established with the assistance of the first-line supervisors. Job applicants have a right to know what is expected on the job prior to being hired; job descriptions can be used in explaining a job to a potential employee as well as existing employees. Further, developing job descriptions in collaboration with the supervisors will mean that the personnel office can more effectively screen the suitability of candidates prior to hiring.

7. Lack of an organized selection process regarding production employees.

    There is no evidence to suggest that anyone is exerting much attention to the issue of selection of production employees. The case presents some insight into the status attached to the selection of employees in general. First, Wilson neglects to identify Walker's position within the company. And second, Walker displays a rather defensive attitude about the nature of his position. Developing an organized system that will specify critical requirements within the selection process is a necessary first step in improving the current situation. A number of specific problems (issues) need attention, such as:

7a. applicants with prior felony convictions;

    Employee application forms need to be revised to ask information concerning any prior felony convictions. Alternatively, a system of background checks might be established. There will obviously be

differences of opinion as to how to resolve
this problem. A clearly defined policy
statement should establish a consistency
of corporate practice and equitable treatment
for all job applicants.

7b. use of and
refusal of
some persons
to submit to
psychological
tests;

Establish (if not already done) the validity
that psychological tests have within this
particular environment. Government regulations typically require documentation of
test validity where "protected group"
employees are involved. If there is no
clear link between performance on these
tests and subsequent job performance, their
use should be terminated. Since there has
been no strong evidence to support the use
of psychological tests, the company should
consider abandoning their use in favor of
a more thorough selection interview.

7c. utility of
polygraph
tests;

Either consistently require the polygraph
test for all applicants or perhaps eliminate
its use altogether. The current requirement
that singles out only blue-collar male
applicants could possibly trigger EEOC
charges against the company. White-collar
crime can be equally destructive to corporate
well-being (especially in view of the involvement with government contracts). The
efficacy of polygraph testing is not clear;
some critics contend these tests may do more
harm to morale than the benefits sought in
decreasing theft. If the polygraph test is
as essential as Walker thinks, consider
utilizing it for job applicants in certain
key positions and perhaps on a random basis
after the point of hire. Since the employment process can raise levels of anxiety for
some applicants anyway, the polygraph test
may not be measuring what it is intended to
measure at the time.

7d. inability to
match people
and positions.

Conduct a job analysis of all the production
positions to establish (via the job
descriptions and the job specifications) an
objective list of job duties as well as a
list of the human characteristics required
for each position. Setting high standards
is commendable but only as long as those
standards are realistic and fair. Assess the
standards in light of new information and
adjust standards where necessary.

8. The application form.

Condense the nine-page application form to a more manageable length. Reassess the relevance of the information being requested with respect to the assembly-line nature of many production jobs. Use the employment interview to gather some of this information, thereby reducing the size and tediousness of the application procedure and securing the advantages attendant to face-to-face interview exchanges.

9. Application review.

Establish a list of objective and standard criteria for selecting individuals to proceed through the selection process. Waiting for an accumulation of applications and then having the personnel staff review them is a drain on an already understaffed situation. Identifying the selection criteria with the use of job analysis information should allow an individual (perhaps a clerk or specialized position) to review applications and maintain a continuous assessment of applications to provide a more timely pool of potential applicants for processing and referral to departmental supervisors.

10. Inadequate employee orientation/ training program.

Implement an orientation/training program that can do the following: eliminate the paper barrage with a more specific introduction of the company's benefits package-- i.e., provide information that is clearly delineated to employees and give them an opportunity to ask questions about those benefits; describe the nature of the work performed by the company and how each employee's department fits into the overall scheme; escort the employees to their respective work areas, introduce them to their supervisors, and follow up a few days later to see how each employee is progressing; instruct supervisors of the importance of introducing new employees to other members of their departments, orienting them to the layout of the work environment, the schedule, work rules, etc.; institute a training/appraisal program that instructs, measures, and follows up performance with feedback to give employees more incentive to perform to their best abilities. Quality is at a premium in this company, and corporate goals are aiming for a 25 percent increase in sales and profits. Neither of these will be attained if orientation and training are inadequate for preparing employees for the jobs ahead.

11. Top management involvement.

Emphasize the importance of top management support for the tasks required of the personnel staff, and stress the important role of the personnel department to assist in the recruitment, selection, and training of new employees. The company needs to attract and keep employees who have the interests and the skills requisite to the nature of the aircraft industry. It does the company a disservice to hire unqualified individuals who probably will become frustrated in an ill-suited environment.

12. Communication within the company.

Inform and involve the employees in the nature of the consultant's work in the company. (Suspicions can create a rumor mill run rampant!) An employee survey (if taken) could provide a wealth of information to the consultant and the company, but only if employees have been informed of the circumstances surrounding the consultant's mission.

The foregoing list is by no means all-encompassing or all-conclusive in nature. Students usually will identify additional problems/issues and develop suggestions for solving them.

NOTE TO INSTRUCTORS

For the instructor who would like to use another broad, comprehensive case similar to this case, we have included in this Instructor's Manual another such case, entitled "Vanzo Manufacturing Company." (See pp. 192 to 210.) The Vanzo case was written by Major Jeffrey A. McNally, who co-authored the "Pacific Aircraft Company" case. Both cases are similar in general thrust and broad scope of personnel/human resources management issues.

CASE 2

THE JORDAN COMPANY

This case involves many important issues. Some of these are as follows:

1. The decision by Jordan to employ a personnel manager.
   a. Who determines the morale of the members of the group: the line supervisor or staff personnel?
   b. How can a staff member affect morale?
   c. Why is morale deteriorating? In fact, how do we know that it is deteriorating? What about the possibility that Jordan himself is the cause of the deterioration of morale?
   d. Does a company with 475 employees need a personnel manager?
   e. Can we expect an organization with 475 employees to behave like "one big happy family"?

2. The decision to promote John Graham.
   a. What are the qualifications required in a staff member?
   b. What are the qualifications required for the position of personnel manager of the Jordan Company?
   c. How well qualified was John Graham?
   d. How well did Jordan define the job to Graham? How many interpretations might you find for the statement, "The scope and success of the personnel department's activities will be pretty much what you make them"? How did Graham interpret this statement?

3. The decision to attach the personnel department to the production manager's office.
   a. How does this affect the ability of the personnel department to serve the other functional divisions of the organization?
   b. Since the personnel department operates at a low level in the organization, with what kinds of problems will it be concerned?
   c. How much help will the personnel department provide to the top management of this organization?

4. The memorandum sent by Graham to the foreman.
   a. Does Graham look upon his role as that of a staff member?
   b. How does this memorandum affect the position of foremen in the organization?

27

5. The complaints voiced by the foremen.
   a. How do you interpret these complaints? Is it possible that the foremen are complaining about the loss of status?

6. The recommendation by the plant manager to abolish the personnel department.
   a. What will happen to John Graham?
   b. Does this company need a personnel department?
   c. What short-range problem do you see arising? What long-range problems?

Typical solutions offered by class or conference members follow:

1. Return Graham to his former position.
2. Allow him to remain in present position, but give him more training and guidance.
3. Place the personnel department directly under the president and at the same level as the plant manager, sales manager, and treasurer.
4. Discharge Graham.

No easy solution for this case exists. It is difficult to return Graham to his former position, since the company presumably has already filled the vacancy; Graham will find it difficult to remain in his present position, since he has lost the confidence and respect of his associates. It will not be easy to place him in a higher position, since he has presumably failed in this one; discharge of an able and enthusiastic employee is painful and costly to the organization.

Normally, the instructor should refrain from divulging the final outcome of a case where it is known, but in this case the instructor may wish ultimately to inform students that (a) Graham resigned from the company; and (b) the company decided to try to get along without a personnel manager. The real-life outcome was not a happy one, either!

The instructor may wish to break up the class or conference group into small groups of six to eight persons and have each group analyze the case and arrive at a recommended solution. The group might be instructed to employ the following problem-solving procedure in making its analysis and decisions:

1. Identify the problems or problem areas.
2. Analyze the problems.
3. Synthesize the various problems in an effort to determine whether or not these are symptoms of other, more basic problems.
4. Identify possible solutions.
5. Evaluate solutions.
6. Adopt the solution best suited to the current situation and the people involved.

THE JORDAN COMPANY

DISCUSSION QUESTIONS

1. If you were John Graham, how would you interpret Mr. Jordan's statement concerning the scope of the activities of the personnel department?
2. What did John believe his organizational position to be? What do you believe it should have been?
3. What are the implications of placing the personnel department under the production manager? Scope of activity? Level of activity? Utilization of staff personnel?
4. How do you explain the reaction of the foremen?
5. If you had been John Graham, how would you have handled this situation?
6. What would you do now if you were Thomas Jordan?

CASE 3

THE MIDVALE PLANT (A):   THE REORGANIZED PERSONNEL DEPARTMENT

In some respects, this case is similar to the Jordan Company case, which is also in this section. However, the Midvale Plant illustrates what happens to an informal personnel function as a result of reorganization and consolidation into a formal personnel department. As in the Jordan Company case, the advent of a formal personnel department seems to have created new problems. This case also offers the opportunity to discuss the problems of the "decentralization of management functions" in a large multiplant organization.

DISCUSSION QUESTIONS

1. Evaluate the role of Miss Martin in personnel administration prior to the reorganization.

2. Evaluate the statement of responsibility and authority for the new personnel department provided by Mr. Hawk, and consider the decentralization of staff personnel work occurring in the case.

3. Why did many of the managers and supervisors view the new personnel department setup skeptically and with reservations? How was this related to the previous informal setup as handled by Miss Martin?

4. At the end of the case what alternatives are open to Tom Jones to improve his situation with each of the following groups?
    a. Company supervisors
    b. Higher management
    c. The union and employees in the plant

5. Outline a course of strategy for Tom Jones that will help to make his new personnel department a more viable part of the company scene.

CASE 4

TRAVERS HOSPITAL: THE PERSONNEL DEPARTMENT SECRETARY

In recent years, numerous hospitals and other health care facilities have been involved in organizing efforts by unions. They are learning that organizational loyalties of individuals often become rather blurred during the course of union organizing campaigns.

In this case, the situation of Nancy Columbus is a delicate one from the management standpoint. Nancy Columbus has been a long-time resident of a relatively small community, and she is very loyal to the perceived needs of her townspeople and friends. But she also occupies an influential position, and she is close to the locus of management decision making. Nancy Columbus does not seem to understand that management's perspective concerning a labor union can be quite different from an employee's perspective, regardless of whether or not management has been guilty of fair or unfair treatment of its employees.

Management must handle this situation in a very sensitive fashion. If management resorts to disciplining Columbus for her communicating the meeting information to other employees, she may quickly become a "martyr," which will further antagonize the sentiments of the employee group. On the other hand, management must be able to protect itself from having all of its confidential meeting information communicated quickly to employees. This is particularly true if management is to engage in some form of counter-union organizational campaign.

DISCUSSION QUESTIONS

1. Evaluate the role that Nancy Columbus played as "mother hen" to employees who had problems. Should Mr. Lyon have disciplined her for serving in this fashion?
2. Why would a hospital management prefer its employees not to join a union? Does this attitude necessarily mean that hospital management is indifferent to employee requests and problems?
3. Evaluate Mr. Lyon's comment to Mr. Warner concerning Nancy Columbus: "I don't think she was distorting most of what we said on purpose. She just doesn't understand the way in which management must operate."

31

4. At the end of the case, what should Mr. Lyon and/or Mr. Warner do regarding Nancy Columbus? Evaluate various alternatives open to them at this point.

CASE 5

UNINTENTIONAL PREJUDICE

The case provides a societal, community context that impacts
upon a manager's approach to a personnel/human relations problem.
The problem facing Richard Wayne was not one of a traditional
production, sales, or marketing orientation; rather it was a
developing human situation that seriously affected the financial
viability of the firm. And the way that Wayne responded to this
situation was hardly one of astuteness or sound judgment.

As owner and manager, Richard Wayne was responsible for the
activities of the employees as well as the operations of the
company. From a human resources management perspective (a perspective he apparently endorses), his task involves coordinating
the functions of management--planning, organizing, staffing,
directing, controlling--in such a way that both the objectives of
the company and the needs of the employees can be satisfied
simultaneously.

However, in this case Wayne at first tries to ignore the
criticism and negative public relations coverage in such a way that
his business continues to suffer. Then he adopts a "compromising"
approach by more or less forcing one of the controversial employees,
John Willet, to resign. Then he further compounds the problem by
having Sheila Harper agree to a dubious arrangement by which she,
too, leaves the firm, only to find that a year later Ms. Harper
decides to sue Wayne for discrimination and unjust discharge.

The case certainly illustrates the complications that can face
a company that tries to mesh both organizational objectives and
individual needs in a haphazard way. Although it cannot be expected
that these dual interests will always coincide, what should
management's position be in those instances when a conflict of
interests exists? At what point do human needs and human concerns
give way to the needs for an organization to survive in the
marketplace? Achieving that critical balance is one of the
challenges of effective personnel/human resources management.

DISCUSSION QUESTIONS

1. How might Richard Wayne have approached the boycotting issue
    differently? Did he have recourse to the courts to prevent

33

interference on the part of the religious groups? Why or why not?

2. Should Wayne have publicly responded to the groups' allegations in an effort to protect his business interests? Why or why not?

3. Would Richard Wayne have been well advised to have terminated both John Willet and Sheila Harper simultaneously? Discuss. (The instructor may wish to introduce in this discussion the legal concept of employment-at-will, which generally holds that employers may terminate employees at any time unless there is some form of actual or implied contract in place.)

4. Evaluate Wayne's arrangement with Sheila Harper to secure her exit from the firm. Why was this undesirable, and how did it leave him vulnerable to charges of descrimination?

5. If the charges of discrimination are pursued, does Wayne have any legal defense against the charges (e.g., business necessity, lack of adverse impact, etc.)?

6. As a general matter, to what extent are the private lives of employees a corporate concern? A liability? Discuss.

CASE 6

THE NIGHT SHIFT GROUP

This case illustrates vividly the importance of human resources management in a hospital setting. An efficient, closely
knit group has been turned into a disorganized, unhappy, and bickering group in a relatively short period of time.

Certainly, much of the fault lies with Paul Seay's approach to
managing hospital personnel. Mr. Seay seems to operate on a Theory
X approach to management by writing memos, making directives, and
following up very closely. He has little faith in his subordinate
managers to follow through in their responsibilities.

But questions can also be raised concerning the role of Mrs.
MacDuff and her night shift group. Mrs. MacDuff failed to measure
up to her supervisory responsibilities; she approached the problem
of the missing linen in a rather indifferent manner. Furthermore,
by becoming so close to her own group, she failed to see her overall managerial responsibilities to the entire hospital.

In this case, as in so many organizational situations, some
consultation, discussion, and effort at cooperation among the
parties involved, particularly the management personnel, could
have avoided this deteriorating situation.

DISCUSSION QUESTIONS

1. Evaluate Mr. Seay's approach to the problem of the missing
    linen.
2. Evaluate Mrs. MacDuff's handling of the situation on the night
    shift.
3. Evaluate the impact of the situation upon the performance of
    personnel on the night shift.
4. What recommendations would you make to the hospital adminis-
    trator as a result of this case?

CASE 7

A BREACH OF CONFIDENTIALITY

This case has been placed in the first part of the text because it well illustrates a number of aspects of the overall personnel/human resources management function. For example, it demonstrates the need for policies designed to promote the mutual welfare of both customers and employees. Second, it shows how even well-developed policies can be subverted by employees who choose to bend policies to their own wishes for their own personal reasons. Third, the case illustrates how human behavior manifests itself at work. Rumors and "grapevine" conversations are well known to most organizations, and these can have a serious impact on the performance of people within an organization. And there is the question of disciplinary action--if any--which may be meted out as the personnel director and management try to sort out the truth.

The instructor has a number of avenues for discussion. One such area is the policy itself regarding confidential materials. Some students will contend that the policy as worded in the new employee handbook is somewhat vague as to meaning. The phrase "violation of this trust" is a rather broad and encompassing term and may be open to varying interpretations.

Then there is the questionable behavior of employee Mary Alton in connection with fellow employee Julie Shaak. Certainly what they did was improper; requesting laboratory work under an assumed name of another employee was a form of dishonesty that should not be condoned.

But most of the case discussion will then turn to the conversations regarding the confidential information about the results of the laboratory test. The following questions should promote ample discussion and debate.

DISCUSSION QUESTIONS

1. How should Personnel Director Emily King and higher management determine who is telling the truth in this situation? Why is this difficult to ascertain?
2. If Julie Shaak is found to have made a false accusation, what should management do? If it is determined that Coleen Luera and Arthur Jacobs did in fact reveal and discuss confidential information, what should management do?

3. Should management take any action against Mary Alton, who used an improper procedure, and any action against Julie Shaak, who was part of this improper procedure? Discuss.
4. Should any action be taken to protect the identity of Mary Alton as the actual employee who had the laboratory test made using another employee's name?
5. What--if anything--should be done to stress again the confidentiality issue among all employees at the medical center locations?

PART TWO

PEOPLE AT WORK

CASE 8

TOM MENDOLA

Tom Mendola's situation is indeed an unfortunate one. As a high school dropout, forced to support a family in poor circumstances, he is placed in a situation not to his liking and to which he cannot seem to adjust. The basic question posed by the case is just how far the management of the Thornton Company can go in trying to salvage Tom Mendola as an employee. Does the company have any responsibility to exert further effort to "save" Tom Mendola in view of the circumstances surrounding Tom's family life? Is a moral issue involved? Some students will believe that Tom deserves another chance. Others will point out that Tom has had several chances already, and that it is questionable whether Tom will respond to another one in the machine shop department. A fruitful avenue for discussion would be to emphasize company policy with regard to training and progression of workers in jobs and situations of this sort.

In the past, the authors often have added a hypothetical issue to this case in classroom discussions. After a period of time, the authors raise this question: "Suppose Tom Mendola was black. Would this make a difference in the way the situation will be handled? Should it make a difference?" With teenage unemployment, particularly black teenage unemployment, of great concern to society, how should companies respond and yet maintain control of their job situation, including the impact on other workers in the company itself? The Tom Mendola situation certainly is one of the most potentially explosive types of personnel problems in modern times, and students should come to recognize that there are no easy solutions for dealing with such a situation either on an individual or a broader societal basis. Yet, solutions must be found.

CASE 9

CARL LOHMAN, LINEMAN

This case offers an excellent opportunity for the instructor to illustrate how the goals and interests of an individual may come into conflict with those of the company for which an employee works.

DISCUSSION QUESTIONS

1. Is a long-service, faithful employee entitled to special consideration?
2. What is the responsibility of management to inform employees of their responsibilities to the company?
3. Is a reversal of a foreman's decision in a case of this type a wise company action? Will the foreman's position be weakened as a result of this reversal?
4. Is the warning by the company and the union likely to solve the problem at hand?
5. At the end of the case, what policy problem still needs to be settled? What steps would you recommend to develop an appropriate policy?

CASE 10

TOO MANY PERSONAL CALLS

    John Dixon probably has regretted his hastily issued memo limiting personal telephone calls to telephones in the lounge area. Although his objectives may have been desirable, his approach to the problem appears rather arbitrary and confusing to the supervisors in the company. Obviously, the supervisors are in considerable disagreement over the whole issue, and they resent the manner in which the directive was given to them by Mr. Dixon.

DISCUSSION QUESTIONS

1. Was Dixon justified in issuing his policy statement on personal calls?
2. Is this a problem of sufficient magnitude for managerial attention?
3. Why had the supervisors not taken corrective action prior to Dixon's memorandum?
4. At the end of the case, outline a series of recommendations to Dixon to deal with the problem of personal telephone calls and to gain support of the supervisors. (Suggestion: Could a participatory management approach be utilized in which supervisors try to develop their own policies in this matter, including different procedures to cover individual situations?)

CASE 11

SEE, WE WERE RIGHT!

Although this case has been placed in the "People at Work" section, it might just as well have been included in Part Three, which focuses on organization. The case illustrates the working of both formal and informal organizations; perhaps it would be better stated that it shows what can happen when the formal and informal organizations are not "pulling together" in the same direction.

The motives of Joe Grant and Bull Jones to save the company a considerable amount of money are to be commended. They follow the normal chain of command, only to receive a disappointing communication that their suggestion would not be used in the plant situation. At this point, Jones and Grant decide to take matters in their own hands, and they do not bother to inform higher management about their decision. At the end of the case their boss, Mr. Chad Hodges, receives a very embarrassing telephone call that is sure to lead to a great amount of acrimony and attention. The following types of questions should encourage considerable discussion among the students.

DISCUSSION QUESTIONS

1. Evaluate the approach by which Joe Grant and Bull Jones made their suggestion concerning the use of the old die. Might there have been a better way to make their suggestion known?
2. Evaluate the manner by which the director of manufacturing, Chad Hodges, forwarded the suggestion to the engineering department.
3. Evaluate the response of the engineering department to the suggestion concerning using the old die. How might the engineering department have responded in a more interested or professional manner?
4. Were Bull Jones and Joe Grant justified in going ahead and adjusting the old tooling and turning out the manufactured parts? Why or why not? What alternatives might they have pursued? (Emphasize that at the very least they should have informed Mr. Hodges of what they intended to do.)
5. At the end of the case, how should Hodges respond to the plant manager, Willis Whitney? What avenues will be open to Hodges to straighten out the situation?

6. In general, what needs to be done at the ABC Company to make sure that both informal and formal organizational behavior patterns work to the benefit of the company in the future? Discuss.

CASE 12

SECRETARIAL FRICTION

DISCUSSION QUESTIONS

1. What do you feel are the underlying causes of the apparent
    friction between Linda and Marion?
2. What options are available to Mr. Albertson regarding his
    secretarial problem? What are the possible consequences of
    each of these courses of action?

    I was employed as a consultant to Mr. Albertson's section
during the time that he decided to transfer the MIS project from
Marion to Linda. Mr. Albertson expected Marion to be somewhat
upset when the task was taken from her. He was willing to accept
some risk of negative behavioral consequences due to the rapidly
approaching project deadline, but the problem developed further
than anticipated.

    It is practically impossible to know with certainty the under-
lying causes of friction between two employees in situations like
this. True feelings will seldom be verbalized, even in counseling
sessions; nevertheless, there appear to be some clues in this case.
It often happens that reducing subordinates' workloads for any
reason is perceived as a threat to their security rather than as
a burden lifted. They may feel as though part of their worth
and/or power has been taken away. This appears to be at least
part of what Marion felt. The age difference between the two women
may have been another factor contributing to the friction. An
older employee sometimes feels threatened by a younger, more aggressive one.

    There are several options open to Mr. Albertson, but as in
selecting among several antibiotics for an allergic patient, each
of them might produce unwanted side effects. He could transfer
Marion to another section. This presumes she is purposely in-
stigating the grief Linda is experiencing. Can he be sure of that?
He might first counsel with her concerning the matter, but this
approach carries a twofold risk. If she is deliberately trying to
upset Linda, she will hide her true feelings. If she is not, any
insinuation to the contrary, no matter how subtle or inadvertent,

---

This teaching note was prepared by Professor Charles W. Boyd
of the Department of Management of Southwest Missouri State
University. Used by permission.

is likely to be resented. Feelings could be hurt, and a loyal employee might be lost.

Passively allowing Linda to find a new job is another possible course of action. If Marion was indeed trying to get rid of a competitor, this option would solidify her power while the section would lose a very promising young employee.

A less drastic option would be to attempt to smooth relations between the two women and hope that they will develop a better understanding and appreciation of one another. The risk taken here is that their relations will continue to degenerate and their unhappiness will begin to infect the other employees. It is difficult to hide a problem of this nature in such a small work unit.

CASE 13

TRI CITY UTILITY COMPANY: A PROBLEM OF ALCOHOLISM

This short case can be used for a number of purposes. The authors have found it particularly useful as an example of a company policy designed to deal with the serious problem of alcoholism on the job.

Some students will argue that a company does not have the right to probe into the personal lives of employees unless an employee's absenteeism, tardiness, or performance dictate that action should be taken. Exhibit 2 of the Johns Hopkins questionnaire will cause considerable discussion. Would employees resent responding to such a questionnaire, even on a confidential and voluntary basis?

Many companies today are concerned about the problem of drug abuse as well as the problem of alcohol. Could a policy such as the one promoted and proposed by Dr. Medico be developed to provide information and assistance to drug abusers or potential drug abusers? Should these types of problems be a matter of company concern, or should they be handled by normal disciplinary procedures? These questions are increasingly of concern to many companies in our society.

At the end of the case, have students decide whether or not they would approve the adoption of the policy suggested by Dr. Medico. If so, what steps should be taken to implement the policy? If not, why not, and what other alternatives might be developed to deal with the problem of alcoholism and/or drug abuse?

ADDITIONAL PROJECT

Many large companies and organizations have implemented Employee Assistance Programs (EAPs) to assist employees with personal problems such as alcoholism, drug dependency, domestic problems, debt, legal concerns, stress, etc. In connection with this case, the instructor may wish to have students research and report on EAP programs (e.g., perhaps by contacting or interviewing personnel in charge of an EAP corporate program) for additional insights into these types of humanistic efforts.

CASE 14

FRAZER'S DEPARTMENT STORE (A): COMMUNICATIONS

This case should be utilized both to illustrate the problem
areas of communications and the integral part played by communications in the total behavioral patterns in a business organization.

Most of the case revolves around the report by George Prentiss. It seems from Prentiss's report that Frazer's uses a considerable number of communications media. But it is also obvious
that some channels are considerably more effective than others.

Accepting Prentiss's report at face value, many questions will
come to mind in the course of this case discussion. Some students
will be quick to point out that the meetings held ten minutes
prior to store working hours, without compensation of the employees, hardly could be effective. Yet management believes that the
employees as a whole do not resent this use of their time.

It is apparent from the report that the counseling program
and the attitude surveys are of limited usefulness. The fact that
the personnel department, rather than the line supervisors, is
doing the rating and counseling of employees is most questionable.
If an attitude survey is to be useful, all employees--not just
those in subpar departments--should be surveyed, and the survey
results should be analyzed carefully and acted upon.

The report reveals the effect of the informal communications
network, known sometimes as the "grapevine," as being (in Prentiss's terms) "the quickest means of communication." Certainly
the instructor should point out that where a strong, well-developed
grapevine is in operation, this in itself may be a clue to lack of
adequate and proper communications in the organization as a whole.
That is to say, where the formal channels do not work properly,
the informal grapevine will try to fill in the gaps.

An interesting exercise is to have students analyze each communications approach and type of media used at Frazer's, discuss
pros and cons, and suggest improvements.

In summarizing the case, the instructor may wish to note that
Frazer's has fallen into the trap, which is a common one in business and industry, of making great efforts to communicate on a
downward basis. That is to say, the communications from management
to employees appear to be sufficient from management's standpoint,
but they may not be sufficient from the standpoint of the workers.

Further, there is little question that the communication system
does not provide for an adequate worker-to-management channel.
The problem of obtaining sufficient feedback is one that deserves
immediate attention, and Prentiss's suggestion for reinstituting
the suggestion-box system might be a step in this direction.

Another avenue for interesting discussion is to consider the
role of George Prentiss and Mr. Stone in this situation. Did
George Prentiss "stick his neck out"? If he did, what is likely
to be the course of action followed by Mr. Stone and Ms. Fiske?

Finally, the instructor should point out--if the students do
not recognize it already--that perhaps the most difficult road-
block to improving communications at Frazer's will be convincing
top management that a problem of poor communications actually
exists. How can this fundamental barrier be overcome? Who will
take the lead in improving the situation? Unless management sees
the problem as a high priority item, it is unlikely that much
improvement will come from Prentiss's efforts.

CASE 15

SAGITT MANUFACTURING

According to his own report, a graduate student in organization behavior was involved in a situation that superbly illustrated the classic human problems involved with introduction of change. This case very much reminds me of the classic Dashman case, which has been in the Harvard Business Review at least two times.

Change is an inevitable process. The implementation of the microfiche program at Sagitt could have been a constructive, efficient time and money conservation method had a few things been done differently.

There are several basic guidelines concerning the change process. They are as follows:

1. If a company wishes to enlist in any change effort that involves or changes individual behavior, the company must include a means by which such changes are carried out. Changes in the behavior of those people who cause the organization to function must occur. In the case of the manufacturing employees at Sagitt, no effort was made by Maisley or any other manager to change the existing behavior of the employees. They had always used paper reports and were not retrained to the new microfiche procedure. Effective change cannot be successful if the employees are not trained for the change.

2. In order for a change effort to be successful, top management personnel have to be motivated and interested/enthused about the change. Maisley, the head of the manufacturing department, was never really behind the microfiche program. Consequently, his employees were not motivated to use the new system.

3. In implementing a change effort the people who are to respond to the change should be brought into the action as soon as possible to help define the problem and solution. This participative approach works best with an educated work force. When the employees are involved in the change process, they are generally more committed to the new program. The employees in Maisley's department were never involved even though the change was directly related to them and their particular job.

This teaching note was prepared by Professor Harriet Stephenson of Seattle University as a basis for class discussion. Used by permission.

4. Successful change occurs when people are informed, especially key management personnel. Grobeschmidt was the only key person at Sagitt who fully understood the program. He did not educate the vice president of manufacturing (Maisley), whose department was directly affected. As a result, the employees were not educated about the new method. Of key importance in implementing a change effort is changing personal behavior. Established patterns of behavior must undergo the following:

   a. Unfreeze (thaw)--A person/group must be convinced that the change is good and needed. The existing behavior patterns need alteration.

   b. Change--Re-educate and retrain the person/group;instruct them concerning the new method.

   c. Refreeze the new information. Reinforcement-operant conditioning can be a way of "setting" new behavior pattern.

   Initiating structure--the extent to which a leader is likely to define and structure his or her role and those of the subordinates toward goal accomplishment is, in fact, what D. Grobeschmidt did with his goal: microfiche. Grobeschmidt defined the problem--escalating paper and labor costs--and formulated a solution--the microfiche program. He isolated himself and his project from key people like Maisley and, subsequently, the manufacturing employees. It does appear that Maisley showed little or no interest and constructive criticism in the entire program. This apathetic attitude added to the deterioration of the entire project.

In summary, we believe that the foregoing change process met with resistance and has been unsuccessful because that change process had the following major deficiencies:

1. Complete lack of user input and coordination with users during the project
2. Users' feeling that the new system was not theirs
3. Users' lack of proper training in the use of the equipment
4. No obvious benefit for the user
5. Complete lack of communication
6. No follow-up by management to monitor progress of the change
7. Adherence to the old ways by implementers of the change not made unrewarding
8. Failure to obtain affected group leaders' acceptance of the change
9. Failure by implementors to obtain the consent, cooperation, or support of those who would use the new system
10. Allowing the change to come as a surprise to the group primarily affected

The data processing manager had hoped to reduce the escalating costs of paper by implementing a new program that would be efficient in terms of reduced material and labor costs. However, the program--as implemented and headed by Grobeschmidt--has resulted in unused microfiche reports and in the use of outdated paper reports, thus causing low morale of employees and inefficient systems of reports.

RECOMMENDATIONS

1. We suggest a normal system follow-up and evaluation of the innovation be conducted jointly by data processing and manufacturing personnel. Determine how well the system is accomplishing objectives and meeting the needs of manufacturing. This is a normal procedure for any large new system. Since the systems analyst in the data processing department is aware of the problem, the difficulties of the innovation could be approached with delicacy.

2. Stop producing paper copies of the microfiched reports. This action can be justified by the purchase of a microfiche viewer which has the additional capability of reproducing single page copies of the required reports. This makes the previous practice of reproducing reports unrewarding, since there will be only one machine capable of giving reproduced paper copies and the time required to reproduce an entire 500 page report would be prohibitive.

3. Conduct an extensive training and familiarization course for all employees having to use the microfiche reports. Get the users to believe in the benefits of the fiche through training and intimate use. The first portion of the training should be directed at the various group leaders among the users. They in turn would have the responsibility for training the other members of their groups in the proper use of the microfiche and viewers. The innovation now becomes less foreign and more of an internal change.

4. Follow-ups should be conducted periodically to insure the acceptance and proper usage of the innovation.

5. Conduct an extensive communications campaign to explain the benefits and advantages of the innovation.

6. Coordinate all of the above and subsequent activities with user management and group leaders.

7. Ensure that there are no more surprises by coordinating all future actions in this area and by proceeding slowly and cautiously with any more changes in this area.

ADDITIONAL COMMENT

Up to this time the data processing manager was concerned with many other priority items. Apparently without pressure, the group slowly increased usage of the microfiche, and the manager has recently received requests from some of the users themselves (manufacturing) to increase the use of microfiche. Also in the future, duplicating and reproduction costs are going to be billed directly to the users, not to data processing and reproduction.

CASE 16

FILMORE ELECTRIC COMPANY (A): THE MACHINE SHOP

The case presents a series of interrelated problem areas, and it might well be included in the wage and salary section. The immediate problem that the case manifests is that of the incentive payment system, which obviously is not working in the machine shop.

Why isn't it working? Several reasons could be suggested.

First, the poorly timed rates set by the time-study department are certainly a major factor. Actually, the poor standards may be a direct result of an inappropriate effort on the part of the company to establish wage incentives in the machine shop. The non-repetitive nature of some work in machine shops is hardly conducive to wage payment on the basis of output. (See the Filmore Electric Company (B), Case 72 for another example in which Filmore was having similar problems due to its wage incentive efforts.)

Second, the actions of the group in pegging production have effectively thwarted the objectives of the plan. This is an excellent example of the "informal organization" countering the objectives of management.

Third, a lack of proper supervision in the shop has contributed significantly to both of the above conditions. One wonders about the quality of supervision, as well as the limited amount of supervision being given in the shop, if the work group has been able to peg production for so long.

DISCUSSION QUESTIONS

1. Should Bill Webster, the foreman, take any disciplinary action in this matter? If so, what should he do?
2. What should be done about the wage incentive plan in the machine shop?
3. What should be done in regard to supervision in the machine shop? Does Tom Horton appear to be a logical candidate for assistant foreman?
4. What organizational changes might improve the shop situation?
5. If you were Mr. Anderson, the superintendent, what course of action would you take in this matter?

CASE 17

THEFT IN THE OFFICE

This case offers a number of areas for interesting discussion. First of all, there is the question of whether a company should be responsible for providing lockers or some other type of secure place where employees may leave their purses and/or valuables. Many employers would contend that they should not be required to do so, since employees are expected to demonstrate honesty and integrity regarding use of company assets. The same expectation automatically would be apparent in terms of property of fellow employees.

But most of the discussion will focus on the handling of the problem by supervisor Veronica Richards and what should be done at the end of the case. Richards's search for the missing wallet, her meetings with Dorothy Friday, and Friday's responses are all ripe avenues for conjecture and controversy. The following questions should stimulate considerable discussion, but it is not likely that there will be unanimous consensus concerning what was done or should be done.

DISCUSSION QUESTIONS

1. Evaluate Richards's search of the office while most of the employees were gone for lunch.
2. Was it a desirable move for Richards to confront Dorothy Friday immediately after finding the wallet? Why or why not? Consider other alternatives that Richards might have utilized.
3. Evaluate Richards's suggestion to Friday that Friday should resign and Friday's responses to this suggestion.
4. At the end of the case, what should Greenberg and Richards do? Consider alternatives.

EPILOGUE

After thoroughly discussing this case, the instructor may wish to share with students the actual outcome of the case including part of a carefully worded letter that was sent to Dorothy Friday. The company decided to terminate Dorothy Friday by relying on the "employment-at-will" concept and without actually accusing Friday of theft. Excerpts from this letter were as follows:

Dear Ms. Friday:

This letter will confirm our meeting in my office
on November 19.

This meeting was to notify you that your employment
would end with this company on November 20. We
reviewed that either the company or the employee
may terminate the employment relationship at will,
with or without cause at any time. You acknowledged
your understanding of the company's conditions of
employment.

You also should know that you are entitled to the
opportunity to appeal your termination to the
next level of management. Should you wish to
appeal your termination to the next level of
management, please forward your reasons to me,
and they will be forwarded to the next level
of management for direct contact with you.

Sincerely,

Veronica Richards

Veronica Richards
Branch Supervisor

Dorothy Friday apparently decided not to carry out her
previous threat to sue the company, since the company did not hear
from her again.

CASE 18

THE CASE OF THE MISSING PICTURES

This case offers an excellent illustration of the problems
encountered in a business organization as it tries to harmonize
the needs and desires of employees while simultaneously working
toward the accomplishment of the goals and objectives of the
enterprise. Chuck Smith is confronted with a situation in which
one of his men--Art Herbert--is unable to function in the work
environment as it currently exists. The problem here is not one
of Herbert's inability to meet the requirements of the job
specification and/or inadequate job performance from a technical
point of view; rather there is a severe conflict of value systems.

In assessing the situation, the class should first try to
identify the pros and cons characterizing Art Herbert's con-
tributions to the organization. On the positive side, he has
a good employment record; he is a conscientious employee; and he
is a graduate electrical engineer (this would indicate that his
skill levels are commensurate with the professional needs of the
firm). On the other side, Art's personal views and values have
isolated him from his co-workers; his actions have involved a
violation of the personal belongings of others (irrespective of
whether or not the pictures were appropriate in the work setting);
he more or less circumvented the chain of command by not following
Chuck Smith's directive to go home; and the situation is requiring
a substantial amount of time from a number of individuals whose
efforts should be directed toward more productive tasks of the
company.

Class discussion can continue with a consideration of the
questions Chuck Smith is pondering at the end of the case. It is
doubtful that the solution reached at the end of the case will be
a lasting one, given the strength of Art Herbert's convictions as
displayed previously.

DISCUSSION QUESTIONS

1. Discuss Art Herbert's contention that the pictures were an
    inappropriate addition to the work environment.
2. Evaluate Paul Downey's initial solution to the problem--
    isolating Herbert from the other eight men in the section.
    Does it matter that all of the individuals involved agreed to
    his plan? Discuss.

3. How might Art Herbert have reacted to this situation dif-
    ferently? What might he have done rather than unilaterally
    taking down the pictures and throwing them away?
4. Discuss Herbert's behavior in ignoring Chuck Smith's directive
    to go home. Was his behavior justified? How will it affect
    his relationship with Smith?
5. The company has gone to great lengths to accommodate Herbert's
    personal beliefs. Is the company obligated to do so? Is it
    sound business/human relations policy to do so? How might it
    affect the morale of the other men in the section?
6. Discuss the strengths and weaknesses of the suggestion to
    transfer Art Herbert to another area of the company.

PART THREE

ORGANIZATION FOR PERSONNEL/HUMAN RESOURCES MANAGEMENT

CASE 19

THE OZARK FOUNDRY

This is an updated version of a previous account of this case
history. Although the dates and certain factual information have
been revised to reflect several contemporary issues, the case data
remain essentially similar to earlier versions. The Ozark Foundry
case thus remains as an excellent study of the difficulties encountered by managers in planning and organizing for the immediate
and long-term future.

The Ozark Foundry has existed for many years, has grown to a
size of nearly 700 employees, and prospects for further growth
appear bright. Yet organizationally, Ozark is operating under
some practices that seemingly are more suited to a company much
smaller in size and expectations.

Students may become so critical of some of the company's
practices and personnel policies--and the person of Mr. Kraft--
that they overlook the significance of the company's successes
to this point. Ozark has survived and prospered in a very competitive business, and its personnel relations have not been seriously deficient even with just a small personnel department.
Consider the significance that most personnel problems still are
handled on an informal basis directly between worker and supervisor. This type of situation is one that many companies would
consider highly desirable. Coupled with the long-service employees
at the company, Ozark has achieved a personnel situation that many
companies never attain even though they have elaborate personnel
policies, pension programs, and major personnel departments.

The key question that the case raises, however, is whether or
not Ozark can continue to operate in its current manner in light
of its outlook for the future. For example, already the company
is experiencing shortages of trained personnel, a problem that
might have been avoided by some careful advance planning.

Renewed union organizational efforts, problems with EEOC and
affirmative action requirements, and the like cloud the personnel
projections of Mr. Grow and other company managers. Unless the
groundwork is laid soon to provide for the anticipated personnel
needs of the company, Ozark will find itself having serious future
employment problems and possibly legal and union challenges.

Writing in Nation's Business, Dr. Eric W. Vetter of Tulane
University has suggested these major ingredients for a sound

61

personnel planning program based on information gathered from forty companies engaged in personnel planning:

1. Start with corporate objectives. Get a clear picture of the company's sales forecasts, profit plan, directions.
2. Take stock of the company's labor productivity rate, employment trends, turnover rates, and the current composition of the professional and managerial staff by age, experience, potential, and so on.
3. Make an annual forecast based on employment trends, manpower availability, and future personnel needs based on the data assembled for 2 above.
4. Plan action programs to implement the forecast in recruiting, selection, development, retirement, and organization.

Dr. Vetter's ideas are directly related to the situation at Ozark Foundry. The matter of corporate objectives is particularly critical in the total planning for Ozark Foundry. Should the company really change its current production and sales approach? If the management decides Ozark Foundry should expand and go after the "mass-produced" markets, what will this imply for financing? For employment projections? For sales strategy? For management itself? And so forth?

DISCUSSION QUESTIONS

1. Analyze the organizational chart of the Ozark Foundry. What changes in organizational structure would you recommend, particularly in view of projections for the company?
2. Is there any value in making estimates of future "minimum personnel requirements"? In the event that the Ozark Foundry's sales should increase dramatically, would a forecast of future "maximum personnel requirements" be of more value?
3. Does the Ozark Foundry need a larger personnel department? Discuss.
4. What needs to be done in regard to the union-organizing effort? The EEOC/affirmative action problem? The need to develop skilled employees?
5. Assume Mr. Kraft has hired you as consultant to the firm. What courses of action would you recommend?

CASE 20

THE CENTER FOR HUMAN DEVELOPMENT

OVERVIEW OF THE CASE

The Center for Human Development is a service organization
consisting of mental health care professionals who are responsible
for providing effective and efficient care to clients from a
four-county area. The organization is a nonprofit corporation
established under the North Dakota Nonprofit Corporation Code and
is dependent for financial resources on federal, state and local
sources.

The organization is headed by its executive director, who is
responsible for the day-to-day activities. The overall policy
guidance is provided by the Board of Directors, made up of members
appointed by County Commissioners.

Historically, the human resource management (personnel)
functions were the responsibilities of the executive director.
In reality, because of heavy workload, the director informally
delegated these duties and the corresponding decision-making
authorities to the division heads and program managers. Thus,
the individual program areas developed their own policies and
procedures pertaining to the personnel functions. The executive
director was kept informed of these decisions.

The control policies established by the various funding
agencies created increasing administrative complexities. To
these were added the absence of a coordinated personnel policy.
The Center began to exhibit inefficiencies. To counter these
symptoms, the director attempted centralization of the personnel
functions and asked the business administrator to supervise the
implementation of these programs. The attempt at centralization
created resentment among the program managers, who had enjoyed

This teaching note was prepared by Professor M. Tom Basuray
of the College of Business and Public Administration of the
University of North Dakota. Used by permission.

63

substantial autonomy prior to this. They began to resist actively the implementation of the new systems. When the executive director attempted to force compliance, the managers began complaining to the legislators. New legislative actions reduced the autonomy of the Center's administrative hierarchy. All the positions within the Center were classified under the state job classification scheme, which resulted in some of the administrative positions, including the executive director's, being evaluated at a lower level. The cumulative dissatisfaction and frustration precipitated the resignation of the executive director, along with some other administrative staff.

OBJECTIVES OF THE CASE

The primary objective of the case is to increase the awareness and understanding by the students of the concept of human resource management as a system and a process. The facts of the case clearly indicate that even though parts of the human resource functions may be performed, even efficiently, by different groups in the organization, the cost of performing these functions soon will surpass any benefits in the absence of an overall, well-coordinated, long-term goal(s)-oriented policy.

The second set of objectives that the case focuses upon is the process that any organization needs to pursue in order to develop an organization-wide set of human resource management policies and procedures. The case is designed to stimulate students' perceptions as to the appropriate locus of decision-making in establishing system-wide human resource policies, the method of implementation, and the control of the process.

The tertiary objective to be achieved is the identification of specific costs and benefits to be obtained from a system-wide human resource management program, as opposed to partial, suboptimal operations of the same.

CASE ANALYSIS

Problems:

The Center for Human Development, at its inception, was a small organization, staffed by professionals who were dedicated to their profession and to the philosophy of service to clients. For the most part, the structure and process of administration were informal in nature. The informality subsequently led to a number of problems described below.

1. The administrators were lacking in their abilities to perceive the nature and significance of the human resource management programs for effective and efficient goal(s) accomplishment.
2. The administrators failed to identify and analyze the organizational environment within which the human resource management programs were to be operating.

3. In terms of the human resource management programs, the administrators of the Center were reactive rather than pro-active.
4. The Center did not possess any evaluative framework to assess the results of the existing personnel policies and practices.
5. The shift from ongoing informal policies and practices to formal was handled inadequately. Unilateral actions requiring compliance from professionals accustomed to autonomous decision-making authority led to resistance.
6. Members of the organization, especially those responsible for implementation and control of personnel functions, were lacking in relevant qualifications and skills.
7. Improper communication and decision-making methods were applied to bring about changes.

Analysis:

     A convenient and effective way to begin the analysis of the case is to conduct a comparative analysis of the existing accounting and financial control system and the human resource management system. The facts clearly indicate that the financial management and control programs at the Center were extensive and highly sophisticated. In comparison, the human resource management programs were informal and weak. One reason for a strong financial and accounting control program is the continuous demands placed on the Center by the resource granting elements in the task environment to insure proper use of funds. The federal, state, and local funding agencies all required rational and sophisticated accountability procedures. However, such was not the case for the human resource management procedures. This exhibits a commonly found syndrome of neglect of the human resource management programs because the costs and benefits are not directly visible and also because appropriate evaluative frameworks are lacking.

     The administrators and staff of the Center were professionals with specialized skills to serve clients. But the organization was deficient in trained and qualified human resource management specialists. This led to the development of simplistic and superficial procedures for discharging the required personnel functions. The responsibilities were informally delegated to the middle level managers in functionally divided groups. Hence, the procedures lacked consistency. However, it did lead to high level of employee satisfaction (as reported by the management consultant) because the procedures, being decentralized, were much more responsive to the employee needs.

     The administrative behavior regarding the development of human resource management programs within the organization was also inappropriate. Payne's decision to centralize the personnel policies and to make the business administrator responsible for their implementation exhibits lack of understanding of human behavior in organizations. The program managers and division heads had been enjoying autonomy in this area. To inform them that such autonomy will be removed/curtailed and centralized under a staff that is perceived by the professionals as being external to the mission group is poor strategy.

The question of centralization versus decentralization of the personnel policies and programs has also not been analyzed properly by the executive director. The facts indicate that the policies shifted from one extreme to the other. The energy and expertise needed to accomplish such a move by overcoming inertia and resistance were not available. Again, one observes an administrative myopia in conceptualizing the process. A mixed strategy of centralization and decentralization would have been appropriate and would have encountered less resistance.

Recommendations:

The immediate task facing the board is the replacement of the executive director. Once the role has been filled, attention is needed in the area of personnel policies and programs. At present, no one possesses the appropriate academic qualifications or skills in this area. Assessment is needed to determine if the organization can afford a staff personnel specialist. The position of the assistant business administrator may be developed into a personnel specialist position. If a full-time staff cannot be supported, then the role can be designed to combine personnel and other functions. The present incumbent may be developed by asking him/her to take courses in personnel areas from the University of North Dakota.

The classification of the jobs in the Center by the State Personnel Department has resulted in lower classification of the top-level administrative personnel. Application for reclassification needs to be made on the basis of rationally developed job descriptions.

In terms of developing a system-wide human resource management program, establishment of a task force composed of program area representatives, the business administrator, and the executive director appears to be appropriate. Such a task force will need to focus on the organizational objectives and, on the basis of these, to establish human resource needs. A manpower planning program is urgently needed. If expertise is unavailable to carry out such activity, help can be obtained from the State Personnel Department.

DISCUSSION QUESTIONS

1. How would you describe the nature and state of the present human resource management system in the Center for Human Development?
2. What are the weaknesses of the present system? What are its strengths?
3. What actions should be taken to deal with these weaknesses? By whom?

4. Could something have been done to prevent the resignation of the executive director? What?

KIRKRIDGE MOUNTAIN LABORATORIES

This case provides ample insights into the problems an enterprise faces as it tries to balance its organizational goals and needs with the goals and needs of the individuals who are part of that enterprise. A number of events that have transpired in this case can serve as a primary focus for class discussion. First is the fact that the laboratories have recently been re-organized into a project (or matrix) style of organization. Although many companies have successfully applied the concept of project (matrix) management, it is also an approach that can create new problems as it solves old ones. Probably the most troublesome problem is that it violates the principle of unity of command. Given the diversity of comments from various members of the administrative staff at Kirkridge, it can be seen that the goals and objectives espoused by one division head will not always be in harmony with those of another who is directing the work of the same employees. Second, the restructuring of the laboratories has resulted in a shifting of responsibilities; this type of situation typically creates tension between those persons who no longer have that responsibility (and authority) and the people now charged with it. Conflicting priorities of plans and even the undermining of efforts of others can result. And third, as a result of his personal business successes, Howard Amer has been selected as the manager to direct the overall operation. A key concern is whether or not the talents and abilities Amer utilized in the past were compatible with the skills needed to improve the laboratories' performance. In conjunction with this is the question of whether or not Amer's new orientation toward the importance of communications and interpersonal relations can translate into a more efficient and productive research environment.

Class discussion can further focus on the following issues: Amer's changed orientation toward the importance of interpersonal relationships and his ability to provide effective leadership; an analysis of his conversation with Dr. Youngblood regarding the future of the Kirkridge Mountain Laboratories; the use and types of required weekly meetings imposed on division and project heads; and Amer's response to Dr. Youngblood's discussion of the Orlow letter. Even more issues are suggested in the discussion questions.

DISCUSSION QUESTIONS

1. Evaluate the contradictions involved in Howard Amer's approaches in his efforts to facilitate improved communications at Kirkridge Mountain Laboratories.
2. Review the characteristics of effective leaders usually described in management textbooks. How does Howard Amer compare?
3. Analyze Amer's use of role playing, simulation games, etc., in the context of the Kirkridge Mountain Laboratories environment.
4. Should Dr. Youngblood have given a copy of Harold Orlow's letter to Amer? Why or why not?
5. Evaluate the differences in perceptions that are illustrated in the comments of Amer and the other administrative personnel regarding the situation at the laboratories.
6. What should Dr. Youngblood do at the end of the case?

CASE 22

THE INTERDEPARTMENTAL TRANSFER CONFLICT

Although this case focuses on a decision that Mr. Detrick must make about Debbie Taylor, there are numerous organizational problems of a real and implied nature that students should be encouraged to define and for which they should make recommendations.

The following Washington University student report analyzing the case should be of assistance to the instructor in preparing and discussing case problems and possible solutions.

CASE PROBLEMS

One of the basic aspects of the transfer situation arose due to a lack of attention to the entire personnel/human resources function. There is no means of providing for the development, transfer, and advancement of employees within the organization.

Development is limited to a departmental basis contingent upon each department manager. Therefore, when the problem of Debbie Taylor arose, there was no predetermined policy or guideline to follow concerning transfers. When Mr. Detrick addressed the problem, he was forced to make his decision based on the specific circumstances with no basis of consistency of decisions of the past. This resulted in his feeling that one or more department heads would feel resentful of any decision. The conflict had grown into a "feud" between the two department managers with the "winner" to receive the employee.

The organizational structure was a simple line structure with its clear, direct relationships. This structure facilitates central control by Mr. Detrick. Yet with 200 beds in the institution, the advantages of line organization in speed and central control are more than offset by the need for specialized knowledge and skill.

The hospital is large enough to warrant additional levels of organization and/or specialists. If there had been a staff personnel department, there would have been hospital policies dealing with transfers. The consideration of Debbie's career might have been on a hospital-wide base instead of strictly departmental. The personnel department would have been specialized in this problem area and could have participated in the early discussions between Mrs. Lewis and Mrs. Morrow. Even though performing a

70

staff duty, the personnel department could offer solutions and alternatives that could benefit both departments.

Due to the lack of departmental coordination, each department manager focused upon her own objectives while the total organizational objectives became secondary. The conflict in departmental goals is in direct contrast to the unity of objective concept. Mr. Detrick, the administrator, must use the theory of organizational balance to determine the priority of his departments. Presently, he is attempting to coordinate all the departments on an equal basis. Each department's objectives should be contributing to the entire hospital's goals in unique manners and degrees.

In dealing with the problem of Debbie's transfer, the two department heads centered on their own departments' needs while not properly considering Debbie's opinion of what she felt was advantageous to her. She wasn't included in the communication between the two department managers. The members of the dietary department wished to ignore that she had more potential than merely carrying out their orders. They failed to recognize that Debbie's need for security in a steady job was supplemented by a set of stronger wants and needs. Debbie wanted social affiliation with others her age and self-respect through a more challenging job that would require her skills and urge her to develop new skills.

RECOMMENDATIONS

Major recommendations to improve management at Mercy Hospital should be aimed at avoiding future conflicts. A staff personnel department should be initiated with a primary purpose of advising the line in staffing questions to achieve consistency of treatment of employees throughout departments. Policies should be instituted in the staffing area to insure consistency and clarity of management's intents.

Regarding interdepartmental transfers, the personnel department should aid the employees in career planning so that people with high aptitudes are not stuck in dead-end jobs.

Another major area is the need for coordination toward one hospital philosophy by all departments. Mr. Detrick should emphasize the interrelationships of the departments and try to promote a unity of objective, a common effort of all the departments working together for better patient care.

In the current situation, I recommend that Mr. Detrick should permit the transfer of Debbie Taylor to the insurance clerk job. He should meet with Mrs. Lewis and Mrs. Morrow to explain that his decision was based upon Debbie's needs and wants as well as her potential. He will have to explain that his decision does not relate to the importance of the business office over the dietary department, but rather upon the career growth of a promising employee. The administrator should assure Mrs. Lewis that another part-time person may be hired in the dietary department to assist her people in peak periods.

Finally, it may be that Mr. Detrick is "spread too thin." I suggest that he consider appointing an assistant administrator to handle daily operations and control minor problems. This would enable the administrator to focus his attention on broader planning and organizing and to work more effectively at achieving hospital-wide coordination of all departments for the overall purposes of the hospital.

CASE 23

THE ADJUSTMENT DEPARTMENT (A): THE ORGANIZATIONAL DILEMMA

Jerry Piatt, a young, college-trained man, has found in the Adjustment Department that answers to human resources problems are not to be found directly in personnel management textbooks.

In this case are interwoven several problems that relate to both the formal organization and the workings of the informal organization. First of all, it is apparent that the technical correspondence section, under its supervisor, Milton Harvey, is a "professional subculture" group that considers itself outside of the organizational structure as it has been developed. Mr. Harvey is prone to ignore formal lines of organizational communication. He does not consider Jerry Piatt as his boss, and he crosses lines of organization in directly criticizing the employees under the supervision of Ms. Bardona.

Students may overlook the fact that Jerry Piatt, in his position as assistant manager, has given tacit approval to the situation as it exists. Jerry must share in the blame for the problems that have arisen, since in the past he has not brought Mr. Harvey into line by insisting upon a pattern of communication in keeping with the formal organization. Jerry also has been guilty of becoming perhaps too familiar with the employees under the supervision of Ms. Bardona. A certain amount of informality in an office is desirable, of course, but if it weakens the position of the supervisor in the eyes of the personnel, it may lead to serious difficulties.

Another important problem area is that of the incentive payment program. Is it desirable in this situation? Perhaps the types of letters to be prepared by the employees in Ms. Bardona's section could be paid for better on an hourly basis. Part of the immediate problem stems from the pressures of time available to the employees in order to make bonus earnings under the payment scheme.

The case has developed a situation where an informally organized group apparently refused to follow the direct order of a supervisor. The problem has been placed in Jerry Piatt's lap, and his future role in this department may well depend on his course of action at this point. Certainly the immediate problem is one that must be dealt with quickly and perhaps sternly. But unless Jerry Piatt is able to come to grips with the overall organizational deficiencies that he has tolerated to this point, his

position as assistant department manager probably will continue
to be a weak one.

DISCUSSION QUESTIONS

1. What should Jerry Piatt do in regard to the immediate problem?
2. What course of action would you recommend to Jerry Piatt to
   correct the organizational problems within the adjustment department? Consider alternatives.

CASE 24

THE ADJUSTMENT DEPARTMENT (B): MANAGEMENT BY OBJECTIVES

This case is a continuation of Case 23, the Adjustment Department (A). Many of the organizational and personnel problems
apparent in the Adjustment Department (A) case are carried over
into operational performance problems apparent in the (B) case.
Mr. Swanson, who is somewhat unknown in the (A) case, has become
convinced that various operational problems are a result of the
organizational conflicts and bickering among members of adjustment
department personnel.

Is "management by objectives" a viable way to approach the
problems in the department? Apparently Mr. Swanson believes that
a good place to start is with Jerry Piatt's position as assistant
manager. Certainly Jerry Piatt has many areas to concentrate on,
and a starting point for improvement might be to develop some specific objectives for his responsibilities.

The Olson's Furniture Stores MBO Worksheet included as a
sample in Exhibit 24-1 of the case can be utilized by students as
a way of approaching Jerry Piatt's assignment. Have the students
develop a list of specific and/or measurable objectives for Jerry
Piatt based on the information provided in both the (A) and (B)
cases. It should be obvious that all objectives cannot be quanti-
fied, so some of them may be in the form of target dates for com-
pletion of certain "projects." Students will find it difficult
to state objectives for Jerry Piatt "concisely and precisely,"
but this is a major element that should be stressed in developing
objectives in any managerial setting.

CASE 25

THE MBO GAME WITH ONE PLAYER

I was employed as a consultant to the Research Section for several matters, one of which was the effort to begin the MBO program. The section director and I both realized from the outset that MBO was not being used on a department-wide basis. Despite the fact that he would be "playing alone," the director felt that this approach would help his employees grow and would improve overall section performance.

Mr. Richards appears to have taken proper steps in initiating the MBO program. First, he educated all of his subordinates concerning the concept of MBO and what it is designed to accomplish. He recognized that the clerks might have difficulty establishing specific objectives since their assignments came almost entirely from the research analysts. They participated in the initial indoctrination so that they would feel some involvement in the new program. The second phase of training involved practice in the writing of objectives. This was an attempt to insure understanding of the nature of good, measurable objectives.

It is very important for students to be able to differentiate among situational factors that are favorable and those which might be detrimental to a new management approach. Some favorable factors operating for Mr. Richards in this case are:

1. His patience with his employees. He recognized the tremendous behavioral learning inherent in moving toward MBO and knew that the process would take time.
2. Careful education of the employees concerning MBO before requiring them to write a set of objectives.
3. The employees' favorable attitude toward MBO, which may be partially attributable to the first two factors.

This teaching note was prepared by Professor Charles W. Boyd of the Department of Management of Southwest Missouri State University. Used by permission.

Factors not favorable to the MBO program include:

1. The lack of support for the MBO program from top management in the department. It is widely recognized that such support is usually vital.
2. Mr. Richards's fellow section directors are not employing the MBO approach. The quotation from Mr. Richards's memo relative to the Data Processing Section points out the importance of integrating objectives throughout the organization.
3. The inherent difficulty of establishing objectives in a nonprofit, service-oriented organization such as the Research Section.

Several options are open to Mr. Richards now that he has been forced by the secretary of the department to deviate from his initial plan of action. He can scrap his section's MBO program and simply revert to past departmental planning practices. This will mark the MBO program as a failure, however, and that may affect the future enthusiasm of Mr. Richards's employees for any new or innovative management techniques. He could regard the secretary's directive as only a temporary setback for his MBO program. A more positive approach might be to consider the five-year objectives his section was required to develop as a broader horizon from which better one-year objectives can be developed. If he decides to continue the MBO program, he might also try to influence his fellow section directors to participate in the approach and integrate the objectives of each section.

It is important for students to see from this case that ideal conditions for MBO do not always exist. The manager must evaluate the positive and negative factors present in his particular situation before deciding whether or not to proceed. In this case, the lack of top management support and participation by other key managers in the department were particularly important obstacles. It is also important to remember that it often takes a longitudinal study of three or four years to judge the effectiveness of an MBO program. Scrapping the concept early has been a commonly reported behavior.

DISCUSSION QUESTIONS

1. What is your opinion of the steps Mr. Richards took in initiating the MBO program?
2. What factors have been favorable to the Research Section's MBO program? What factors have been unfavorable?
3. What course of action should Mr. Richards take now that he has submitted a set of five-year objectives to the secretary?

CASE 26

HOW HIGH THE DOC?

ASSIGNMENT

What would you do in Ms. Barret's position?

Discussion

This case deals with a very sensitive problem in hospital administration—the drinking doctor. To even mention the problem to a superior puts the head nurse, Ms. Barret, in an extremely difficult situation. She must make a judgment about the abilities of a physician who outranks her in prestige and training. The problem is further complicated by the fact that the man is near retirement age, may be able to perform his duties satisfactorily during his remaining tenure, and may offer past service as an excuse to cover up his possible malfeasance.

As far as what Ms. Barret might do, her options are greatly limited. Her alternatives are rather poor:

1. Ignore the situation and do nothing.
2. Present the problem to the chief of staff strictly on her own.
3. Present the problem to the chief and/or the superintendent using other staff members to corroborate her story.
4. Talk to Dr. Collins herself.
5. Request a transfer for herself.

Thus, as in many cases in organizational behavior, she is caught in a dilemma testing both her personal ethics and her interpersonal skills.

Ms. Barret provides some interesting insight into her feelings about the situation:

> I was faced with the problem of a large amount
> of responsibility but no authority. The surgery
> patients and personnel are my direct responsibility
> but I have no authority over many situations. I
> have no authority over the doctors or their

This teaching note was prepared by Professor Richard B. Chase of the Graduate School of Business Administration of the University of Southern California. Used by permission.

activities. My subordinates are aware of my lack
of authority, so rather than come to me with their
problems they find other ways of resolving their
conflicts such as being absent from work or quitting
altogether in hopes of finding better working conditions. Doctors are often seen in staff positions
rather than line but they are the ones possessing
the authority.

Some things that might be done organizationally include the
following:

1. Open lines of communication between the head nurse and the
   chief of staff. The head nurse should be made to feel that
   she can bring up this type of problem without fear of re-
   crimination. Obviously, she feels insecure about discussing
   the problem with the chief of staff, and it may take a major
   change in organizational climate to do this.

2. Bring doctors under line authority of the hospital superintendent. As it is now in Mountain View, physicians operate in
   staff, rather than line, capacity. Hence, it is difficult to
   bring to bear formal authority to correct personnel problems.
   The superintendent is in charge of coordinating all hospital
   services, yet the prime skills--those of physicians--are not
   directly under his control. This seems undesirable.

3. Ms. Barret should be given authority commensurate with her
   responsibility. Specifically, she is in charge of a nursing
   team, yet the physicians have the final say as to its composition.

The data for this case was supplied by a head nurse at a general
hospital.

CASE 27

TOO MANY BOSSES

Many organizational cases present situations where lower-level workers or supervisors skip proper lines of organization in communicating upward to higher levels in a company. In "Too Many Bosses," there is the reverse situation of a boss skipping his supervisors in communicating directly to workers at the lower end of the organization. This type of situation is usually a difficult one to solve for the supervisors and individuals directly affected.

Fred Larson is clearly in a problem position. His position as foreman is being undermined by the actions of the division superintendent, Jess Bradley. The position of Phil Hawthorne also is being weakened. There is little reason to doubt that the morale of the workforce as a whole is affected adversely, since there are few things so discouraging to a worker as uncertainty about to whom he or she is directly responsible.

But how does a subordinate go about telling his boss or his boss's boss to "mind his own business," or words to that effect? There are a number of alternatives open to Fred Larson: Fred could air his complaint to Phil Hawthorne, but Phil Hawthorne may be reluctant to take the matter any further. If Fred Larson would go directly to Jess Bradley, he would place himself in the un-comfortable position of by-passing Phil Hawthorne and perhaps incurring the wrath of Jess Bradley.

As a class exercise, the instructor might have the students list these and other alternatives open to Fred Larson and, in addi-tion, have them cite the advantages and disadvantages associated with each alternative. There will probably be considerable dis-agreement among class members in their selection of the "best" alternative as the course of action for Fred Larson to follow.

CASE 28

OSCAR METZ TOOL COMPANY

This short case is illustrative of problems of organization
and perception of organizational structure on the part of members
who work in different departments and different shift groupings.
The three organizational problems revealed in the preliminary in-
vestigation stated at the beginning of the case unquestionably
are related to problems of perceptions of organization in the shop,
production control, and night-shift groupings.

Probably the most interesting way to handle this case is to
have students try to develop an organizational chart based on the
information provided by the various people in the plant. This
effort will produce a number of inconsistencies, overlappings, and
confusing issues of responsibility and authority.

Have various students in a class compare the organizational
charts of the Oscar Metz Tool Company that they have developed.
This should illustrate how difficult it is really to understand
organizations from simply a chart standpoint. It will illustrate
further that charts per se are not nearly so important as the
understandings of people in an organization concerning how they
relate to each other, and what this means in terms of overall
performance.

At the end of the case discussion: (1) Have students try to
develop an overall "model" chart that they believe will clear up
much of the confusion in the company; and (2) develop policies
and procedures by which people in the company can be informed as
to the proper organizational relationships, and as to how organizational lines should be followed in day-to-day activities.

CASE 29

THE STOW TRIBUNE COMPANY (A): THE BETTER IDEA

OBJECTIVE OF CASE

o To illustrate a situation in which an organization's failure to
   develop new leadership, understand cost/revenue relationships,
   and introduce the necessary innovations has led to financial
   and administrative crises

KEY ISSUES

o Organizational efficiency and effectiveness
o Human resources utilization
o Management of resources

     The case illustrates a situation in which laissez-faire manage-
ment, benevolent paternalism, and resistance to change threaten the
future of the organization. These failures are magnified by the
fact that this nonunion shop is situated in a highly competitive
and cost-sensitive industry where many innovations have been intro-
duced in an effort to offset rapidly increasing wage, newsprint,
and paper costs. Although the discussions relate to the specific
experiences of Terry Kinnear, the state of the company must be
evaluated by the case reader.

DISCUSSION QUESTIONS

1. Do you think Terry's idea was a good one?

    The idea suggested by Terry does appear to be a good one.
    It seems that management spent more time reprimanding Terry
    than it spent in evaluating the idea's merit. Deadline days
    are long hectic days that require the manager to utilize his
    people efficiently. The old way of handling errors is blatant-
    ly inefficient.

     This teaching note was prepared by Professor George E. Stevens
of the College of Business Administration of the University of
Central Florida. Used by permission.

2. Are factors other than cost savings relevant to those evaluating the idea?

   Yes, Terry's idea involves a shift in power. The newsroom under Mr. Roedder is responsible for making copy-correction decisions. Terry's idea places this decision making under Mr. Godfrey. Little attention was directed to the issue of cost savings. It does seem that Terry had taken the time to think through his ideas and was willing to present these ideas to management. The reaction of Mr. Godfrey to the idea suggests that he had not known about the idea prior to his conversation with Mr. Loeffler. There does not appear to be a method (suggestion box, for example) for the formal presentation of ideas aimed at improving organizational efficiency and effectiveness.

3. What approaches or strategies could Terry have used in gaining support for his idea?

   Any number of approaches come to mind. Terry committed a faux pas in going directly to the president. One must question his judgment or his intent. Few people look favorably on a subordinate who puts the superior in the awkward position Mr. Godfrey faced. A more direct approach would have been for Terry to have talked with his immediate superior. A second approach might be to have had those individuals directly affected by present procedures (compositors and proofreaders) discuss the situation with Mr. Godfrey.

4. Should Mr. Loeffler have rejected the idea?

   No, although it may have been appropriate in a structured organization to request that the idea go through channels. But having listened to Terry's idea, it seems appropriate to evaluate the idea on its merit. The justification Mr. Loeffler offers for not accepting the idea suggests an incredibly strong resistance to change. The longevity of the procedures in use does not make them sacred. Finally, such a reaction to suggestions would tend to discourage others.

CASE 30

THE T. R. MILLER SLIPPER COMPANY

There is an old but ever true principle of organization called
the "principle of organizational stability," which advocates that
an organization should be able to survive the loss of any of its
members. This is sometimes referred to as the "indispensable
person" principle; that is, no company should be vulnerable to loss
of an indispensable individual.

It appears that Mr. T. R. Miller has become just such a person
in his own company. This is not an uncommon predicament for small
to medium-sized firms, which often are successful primarily because
of the efforts of one key person. But Mr. Miller has failed to
develop either a successor or a strong management team to carry
on in his absence or demise. Mr. Miller's plan to turn over operating management to an executive committee has floundered, and he
needs to divest himself of an active role in his company as soon
as possible. What should he do? The following questions should
help to stimulate discussion of the case.

DISCUSSION QUESTIONS

1. Why did the executive committee not work out as intended?
2. What solution would you prefer if you were one of the four
    managers who served on the executive committee?
3. What suggestions would you make to Mr. Miller if you were an
    outside consultant brought in by Mr. Miller to advise him
    accordingly?

PART FOUR

SELECTION, TRAINING, AND DEVELOPMENT

CASE 31

FRAZER'S DEPARTMENT STORE (B):
A COLLEGE SENIOR VIEWS THE EMPLOYMENT PROCESS

A major point of this case is one that students may perhaps
overlook. It is that first impressions often are the most significant and lasting ones.

From the case information available, many students will conclude that Mr. Stone, the personnel manager, is a very inept, rude
individual and that Ms. Willoughby, the training supervisor, is a
gracious and charming person. This may or may not be the case.
It is possible that Mr. Stone had a bad day or that his manner of
interviewing was somewhat weak. However, the important fact is
the impression that Mr. Stone left with the college senior. How
often do supervisors forget that first impressions are often lasting ones and that starting a new employee off on the right track
can do much to influence the employee's later ideas and actions.

There appears to be a need for a formally organized induction
program at Frazer's. The only real training available was given
by Ms. Willoughby, and this was more a training in techniques than
one designed to ease the transition period for a new employee coming to an unfamiliar job.

The instructor may wish to make the following assignment in
connection with this case: Assume that you have been hired as a
consultant to Frazer's to recommend improvements in the interviewing and induction programs of the company. What would you recommend?

CASE 32

ELMYRA FRIEDMANN, PH.D.

This case well illustrates how _not_ to go about the recruitment and selection process, particularly for professional personnel. In discussing and analyzing this case, the instructor should have students first define the errors of omission and commission that the various university administrators were involved in and, second, recommend what steps should be taken to improve the recruitment and selection process in the future.

COMMENTARY

Mustang University used an unsatisfactory process when hiring Elmyra Friedmann. The positions for which she applied were re-announced only one month before the beginning of the fall semester. This may suggest that administrators of Mustang University placed a rather low priority on hiring business faculty. Since the reannouncement generated only one applicant for two positions, something must be faulty in the vacancy announcement procedure. Among possible explanations are that the reannouncement may not have been properly targeted to reach those with appropriate academic qualifications; that the reannouncement may have been made so late that all reasonably qualified individuals had previously accepted employment for the academic year; and that the policies and reputation of Mustang University may have discouraged qualified individuals from applying. The fact that Dr. Friedmann was hired without being interviewed on campus by several different persons suggests more concern on the part of high-level admin-istrators of Mustang University about hiring a person on short notice than concern for selecting a qualified applicant who has a reasonable chance of being successful in meeting the demands of the vacant position.

Major parts of this teaching note were prepared by Professor James Calvert Scott of the College of Business of Utah State University in Logan. Used by permission.

88

To improve its faculty-selection process, Mustang University should develop a step-by-step approach similar to the one briefly described below:

1. Develop a job description and specifications for each vacant position.
2. Develop selection criteria based on the job specifications.
3. Identify the likely sources of prospective job applicants.
4. Identify the appropriate methods and media for contacting prospective applicants.
5. Begin recruiting efforts as early as is feasible.
6. Recruit qualified prospective applicants actively.
7. Screen applicants carefully against established selection criteria.
8. Invite highest-ranking applicants to campus for interviews with the departmental faculty, the departmental chairman, and the dean of academic affairs.
9. Make competitive offers to the best applicant(s) in terms of such factors as salary, teaching load, rank, and tenure.

SUBSEQUENT DEVELOPMENTS

This case is actually the first part of a series of unfolding events involving Elmyra Friedmann, Ph.D., and Mustang University. Professor Scott, the author of the total case of Elmyra Friedmann, has provided the following summary of what subsequently happened:

Elmyra Friedmann is quickly hired at a late date by Mustang University to teach business administration classes. Her students register complaints within days of her arrival on campus. Dr. Friedmann accuses several people of tampering with her mail. Since the department chairman is not handling matters to the satisfaction of the dean of academic affairs, he attempts to resolve the problems. During the spring semester Dr. Friedmann is assigned to teach a course for which she has insufficient academic preparation. Problems quickly develop, and a student files a lawsuit against Mustang University for allowing an unqualified instructor to teach. Dr. Friedmann is removed as instructor of the class. Her behavior becomes increasingly abnormal. Ten days before the end of the semester, she is terminated in a manner that violates provisions of the Mustang University faculty manual.

It can be seen from the summary provided here that the hiring of Elmyra Friedmann, Ph.D., proved to be a "disaster" at Mustang University and that the faulty recruitment and selection process was the major precipitating factor in the overall situation.

NOTE TO INSTRUCTORS

Instructors who would like to have the additional parts of this case may write the case author, Professor James Calvert Scott of the College of Business of Utah State University in Logan, to request copies accordingly.

CASE 33

SIMMONS RETAIL CHAIN STORE: SELECTION OF AN AUDITOR

Harry Jamison, the employment manager of Simmons Retail Chain Store, is faced with an immediate problem of whether to consider hiring a man with a prison record. The pressures of a shortage of qualified auditors will lead some students to conclude that it would be worth the gamble to talk to the man who placed the want ad. This is a questionable conclusion, since it would represent (1) an expedient approach, (2) a contradiction to company policy, (3) an attempt to solve an immediate shortage of auditors.

Mr. Jamison has been brought into this situation partially because of the overall problem that the case presents.

DISCUSSION QUESTIONS

1. Is the policy of hiring only experienced accountants a sound policy?
2. Does the company really understand the problem resulting in the high turnover of its auditors?
3. Can a company afford to pay less than prevailing rates for a job that admittedly has certain undesirable features?
4. Under what conditions should a company consider the employment of individuals with prison records?

What is needed is an immediate recruitment program to attract qualified, experienced people to fill current positions. Whether the company can afford to take a chance with a known embezzler is open to debate. The long-run problem, however, is one of establishing a program for recruiting and training accountants for extended service. This may require a complete overhaul of current hiring policy.

CASE 34

PARAGON PULP AND PAPER COMPANY, LTD.

This is a useful case to illustrate a number of factors on how personnel selection should not work. There are several considerations involved:

1. Legal aspects: Can management exercise this type of prejudice (toward age, alcoholics, handicapped persons, etc.)?
2. Business aspects: Is management being unreal in its approach to hiring, or are they being realistic with reference to the type of individuals they feel will do the work required?
3. Organizational changes: Is it possible for the organization to change? The office manager acts as personnel manager. Should the personnel function be separated?

This case lends itself to a general introduction and review of personnel selection procedures. The instructor may wish to spend some time considering the general approaches to the selection process and then check Paragon's system against the list. Thus, a general approach would involve the following:

1. Employee inventory--continuous, sporadic, etc.
2. Recruitment--internal and external; sources of new employees
3. Selection--interviews, reference checks (mail or phone); credit checks, use of tests
4. Training program
5. Corporation structure

General questions may include the need for a formalized approach to interviewing versus unstructured; questions on the number of employees required; who should make the selection; part played by prejudice and basis in selecting employees.

This teaching note was prepared by Professor William A. Preshing of the University of Alberta. Used by permission.

CASE 35

AJAX ELECTRONICS COMPANY: THE PROJECTIVE TESTS

As personnel manager, Art Johnson finds himself in a dilemma with his headquarters personnel staff in Chicago. Headquarters believes that projective psychological tests are important tools in evaluating supervisory and managerial candidates. Art Johnson, however, is opposed to their use, presumably on both professional and legal grounds. The appendix to the case provides some information about the Rorschach and Thematic Apperception tests. These tests must be carefully administered and evaluated by trained psychologists or psychiatrists. Even so, there is some question as to the validity of the meanings that are generated from such tests. Most authorities believe that these tests provide useful information, but that any use of them in personnel selection should be done carefully and in addition to considering all other information that is available.

Art Johnson's concern about the use of such tests in regard to equal opportunity employment considerations appears very justi-fied. The Equal Employment Opportunity Commission has insisted that all tests must show a reasonable degree of validity in pre-dicting job performance. There does not appear to be any evidence that the Ajax Electronics Company has made any effort in this re-gard at this point.

At the end of the case, what should Art Johnson do? Should he try to persuade higher headquarters to change its position, or should he acquiesce to the decision made by higher management?

Another useful way of approaching this case would be to out-line a course of action for Art Johnson and/or company headquarters by which they might try to validate the usefulness of these tests in predicting job performance, including that of minority and fe-male candidates.

CASE 36

RED DOT DRUG STORES: THE POLYGRAPH TEST

This relatively brief case involving the use of the polygraph
test is both interesting and controversial. Many companies, particularly in the retail field, have been using the polygraph test
as a way of trying to reduce employee theft. Typically, polygraph
tests are given regularly to applicants and periodically to existing employees. The four cases cited in the case are quite familiar
incidents to companies that have utilized the polygraph test.

The use of the polygraph test has been very controversial.
A number of states have outlawed the involuntary use of polygraphs
on employees. Yet, many companies similar to Red Dot Drug Stores
believe that the use of the polygraph has been very helpful in
reducing employee theft. What is the proper trade-off between
reduction of employee theft and the questions of employees' privacy,
self-incrimination, and the problem of deteriorating employee
morale?

At the end of the case, have the students develop a plan or
course of action by which Mr. Danford can make a proper decision
concerning whether or not to continue the use of the polygraph
test in his company.

CASE 37

HARRY SIMPSON, SALES MANAGER

This case will elicit considerable student discussion, particularly from those students who are interested in careers in
marketing and sales management.

Harry Simpson seems to be caught up in a series of interrelated problems, some of his own making and some that have been
imposed on him by others. It is clear, however, that Harry has
been approaching his staffing responsibilities on a rather haphazard basis and that this approach has led him into his present
predicament.

Probably the most useful way to use this case is first to
have the students determine all of the problems that they can
identify, both of a specific nature and from a policy point of
view. Then the students should be asked to outline how they would
have Mr. Simpson handle and/or approach the five items at the end
of the case, again both specifically and from a policy standpoint
where appropriate.

CASE 38

THE TRAINING MANAGER'S OBJECTIVES

At first glance, the student reading this case may be confused as to what actually is the problem posed by the case. But anyone knowledgeable about the management-by-objectives (MBO) approach will soon observe that the two human resources managers at Mid-America Insurance Company are not practicing what they apparently are preaching. Bill Green and his boss, Tom Davis, have gone over a number of areas of Bill Green's general responsibilities for training. They are considering conducting an MBO course for other managers in the company. Their own approach to setting up objectives, at least from the information in the case, is very general and lacking in specific targets, which are at the heart of a good MBO program. In other words, it is difficult to see how Green and Davis will be able to sell MBO to other managers, until they state their own objectives in a more clear-cut and specific manner.

A good way to use this case is to have the students develop for Bill Green a list of specific objectives that he could utilize in running his department. For a sample of how objectives might be stated, see Exhibit 24-1, in the Adjustment Department (B) case. For those who are not familiar with the MBO target-setting process, students should be reminded that objectives must be measurable or verifiable--that is, they must include some criteria for accomplishment.

Another major problem that students should be asked to consider is, how should a training department try to "sell" MBO to other managers? Management by objectives is an excellent management approach if it is supported by management people and given total commitment through accomplishment. Otherwise, MBO can be just another exercise in paperwork.

NOTE TO INSTRUCTORS

For background reference material on MBO, see the sources suggested in the Appendix section of Case 24 in the book.

95

CASE 39

THE RAMBUSCH COMPANY

The case presents an opportunity to discuss the issue of
management development and promotion as coupled with a controversial
personal/social matter. A firm's survival depends on its selection
and development of a strong management team whose direction and
expertise will guide an enterprise toward the realization of
corporate goals and objectives.

In this case, the Rambusch Company through Gilbert Winston
is offering Louis Dashman the chance to avail himself of an opportunity for further executive advancement. The question facing
Dashman is whether his decision should be influenced by purely
professional/business considerations or whether Winston's personal
lifestyle and commitment to his outside associations should be a
factor in this decision. Class discussion should include an
identification of Dashman's professional goals, the opportunities
presented at Rambusch given the company's growth potential, the
specific possibilities being presented to Dashman through his
association with Winston, and the impact (if any) that Winston's
personal life may have on the situation and on Dashman's future
management career.

DISCUSSION QUESTIONS

1. Discuss the board's unanimous decision to promote Winston to
    the position of president. Was this a decision based only on
    an assessment of his professional credentials? Do you think
    the board was aware that Winston was gay? If not, should
    that be a consideration in the board's decision given the nature
    of the clients the company serves? Why or why not?

2. If Winston decides to follow through with the press conference,
    what impact will it have on his future with the company?
    Would it make a difference if the company were located in San
    Francisco, New York, or Chicago? Discuss.

3. There appears to be some curiosity and problems surrounding
    Winston within the company ranks. What might he have done
    differently to redirect that curiosity? Or was Winston's
    private life nobody's business but his own, as he said? Does
    his stature in the company make any difference in this regard?

4. Analyze Louis Dashman's concerns that the circumstances surrounding Winston's personal life may affect his (Dashman's)
   future with the company and his relationships with the other
   employees in the company. Are attitudes toward gay persons
   changing, or is there still hesitation among many people to
   accept gay persons on the same professional/managerial basis
   as others who are not gay? Discuss.

5. Discuss Dashman's position from the standpoint of his loyalty
   to Winston. Does Dashman have any obligation to Winston?

6. Discuss the role that merit/expertise/professional qualific-
   ations/past performance play in management promotions versus
   the role that other factors have in such decisions.

7. At the end of the case, if you were the professor, what would
   you advise Louis Dashman to do?

CASE 40

LEAVE OF ABSENCE

OBJECTIVES

   This case aims to:

1. Stress the need for predetermined personnel policies;
2. Manifest the importance of clear, unobstructed, and concise
   communications;
3. Illustrate, through a simple real-life situation, some of the
   potential implications of poorly administered personnel
   policies.

STATEMENT OF THE PROBLEM

   A lack of information, arising from poor communications plus
an inability and unwillingness to describe the exact problem
dimensions, leads to a wrong decision. What are the basic rules
that if properly implemented will prevent similar future unfortunate situations?

DISCUSSION QUESTIONS

1. Study the origin of the promotions problem. How could it have
   been avoided? Who was at fault?

2. List the possible options that the engineering manager has:
   a. before making any announcements on promotions;
   b. after the incident with the personnel director and his
      refusal to intervene.

3. Consider yourself in the position of the engineering manager
   (new in the corporation, basically design oriented, etc.).
   What would you have done differently? What kinds of information (and from what sources) would you seek?

   This teaching note was prepared by Professor Joseph Leonard
of the School of Business Administration of Miami University
(Oxford, Ohio) and Professor John Thanopoulos of the College of
Business Administration of the University of Akron as a basis for
class discussion and analysis. Used by permission.

4. Does Martin have any grounds (legal or otherwise) to stand on if Jim is promoted before him?

5. Explore the issue of Black's responsibility in decision making outside of his professional expertise. What are his added obligations because of his present management post?

6. Study the origin of the promotion problem in the corporate framework. Expand on the areas of lack of coordinated policies and complete communication lines. Make a list of guidelines that should prevent future similar incidents.

7. Comment on Black's remarks to both Towne and Parker. What effects (both direct and indirect) might these remarks have on the case?

SUGGESTIONS FOR ANALYSIS

It is often the case that experienced practicing managers make serious mistakes during their first years in a new working environment. This is often due to the fact that both they and the corporation have set ideas, and it is difficult to accept changed patterns of behavior. Often effective communication is impaired because of problems of clarity, feedback, channel noise, by-passing, filtering, etc.

There are many alternative solutions that could be effectuated, such as:

1. Promote Jim on July 1 and Martin on September 1, explaining to Martin that Jim's seniority was not affected by the leave of absence.
2. Promote both men on August 1.
3. Promote both men on September 1.
4. Reverse the decision and promote Martin on July 1 and Jim on September 1, telling Jim his leave of absence set back his seniority.

There are, of course, many more possible solutions. In actuality both men were promoted on July 1. The Engineering Department was able to avoid an over salary expenditure by delaying the hiring of replacement employees. Thus both Jim and Martin were satisfied and continued to be good employees. George Babb was never told about the incident, and CSI policies were not changed whatsoever. Still, a central question remains—what are the implications for the engineering manager after the silent resolution of this confusion? We may guess that sometime he will have to pay for the mistake. How? When? Internal politics and power structures will dictate the outcome.

Further, we propose that this case may be utilized for class discussion of the following type of questions:

1. What are the pros and cons of company-wide personnel policies?

2. How can the term "experiential isolation" partially explain the described problem? How can this situation improve a communication process model?

3. How does one judge that four key managers meeting after hours and off the company facilities can reach a joint decision?

4. Contingent to the fact that Martin and Jim are not unionized, is it reasonable to assume that the nonunion employees are under the same personnel rules as the union employees?

5. How does one evaluate the fact that a departmental manager announces a promotion decision without prior expressed approval of the personnel director?

6. Does the engineering manager know the meaning of the word "empathy"?

7. How might CSI's organizational climate and morale be affected by the ultimate decision concerning Jim and Martin's promotion dates?

CASE 41

PETRI CHEMICAL COMPANY (A): THE PROMOTION OF KENNETH ROGERS

The instructor will find that this case stimulates discussion of such problems as leadership philosophy and technique, supervisory responsibilities and duties, delegation of work, introduction of change, promotion, status, company policy, and collective bargaining.

DISCUSSION QUESTIONS

1. How do you explain the behavior of the carpenters on Monday morning? Would you have anticipated such behavior?
2. What do you think of Barnes's decision not to consult with Counce about his successor?
3. What do you think of Barnes's decision to post the announcement on the bulletin board on a Saturday morning?
4. How do you appraise the leadership qualities of Rogers?
5. How do you evaluate the decision of the company to place the carpenters under the leadership of the foreman and the riggers?
6. Evaluate Article VI.
7. How would you have made the announcement to the carpenters? What, if any, special attention would you have given to Robert Mangrum, Joe Emery, and Wilbur Schuh?

CASE 42

PETRI CHEMICAL COMPANY (B): HARRY THURMAN

This case points up the problems associated with assessing the performance of people. The supervisor in this case retains an employee who gives every evidence of incompetence; he also gives the employee ratings of "satisfactory" under the company's formal rating system. The supervisor refuses to promote the employee, claiming that he is unable to perform the work in question. The employee, with the backing of his union steward, files a grievance claiming that his long service and ability entitle him to the promotion.

DISCUSSION QUESTIONS

1. Why did the supervisor retain Thurman on the job in face of the evidence of incompetence?
2. What kind of action would have been appropriate with respect to Thurman? When should such action have been initiated?
3. Why would a supervisor give an unsatisfactory employee a satisfactory rating?
4. How would you handle the situation at this point?

This incident is excellent for role playing a grievance meeting. An aggressive union steward and Harry Thurman can dramatize both the difficulties and importance of thoughtful evaluation of people. The students assigned to role play the management side will experience difficulty in defending their position.

For further information concerning the nature of the Petri Company, refer to Petri Chemical Company (A), Case 41.

PART FIVE

EQUAL EMPLOYMENT OPPORTUNITY

CASE 43

GLOBAL UNITED (A): MELBA MOORE

This case situation in a large company is significant in relationship to the overall problems of integrating a work force.
The text material of the book discusses the socialization of workers
of different races and ethnic origins. Certainly socialization is
a major part of the overall equal employment opportunity problem,
and the case of Melba Moore illustrates it well.

Blacks tend to be quite sensitive to incidents in their work
situations that they consider to be discriminatory in nature. From
management's standpoint, these irritations may not be considered
race-related, but it is difficult to convince some black workers of
that.

Melba Moore's fears are heightened by the fact that her co-
workers do not attend her party. She states: "This shows again
that the whites in this department are against me and don't care
about my feelings." How can feelings of this type be mitigated?
There may or may not be truth to Ms. Moore's statement. But, in
any case, she believes that discrimination is involved, and it will
be most difficult for her supervisor, Tom Schmitt, to convince her
otherwise.

On the other hand, are Melba Moore's problems more related
to the fact that she is personally ill-suited for the buyer's
position? Was she given the proper training and counseling by her
supervisors before she assumed this very demanding job? Discussion
on these questions will usually prove to be quite controversial.

At the end of the case, what alternatives are open to Tom
Schmitt? Should he try to counsel Ms. Moore again, or would he
be better advised to stay out of this particular situation, if he
can? This is a most perplexing situation.

CASE 44

GLOBAL UNITED (B):   THE OLDER SUPERVISOR

Although this case is a number of years old, it illustrates the problem a company faces in trying to get its supervisory people to follow a nondiscriminatory hiring policy. All of the evidence available to manager Grace Tyson concerning Assistant Manager Bess Goodman suggests that Bess Goodman has discriminated consciously or unconsciously against black applicants. There is a danger in "playing the numbers game" in any examination of minority employment, but the numbers and the incidents involving Bess Goodman point to a serious problem in this regard.

What should Grace Tyson do? Bess Goodman will be leaving the company in several years, at which time her part in the problem will literally fade away. However, can the company afford to wait several years? As pointed out in the Global United (A) case, the company has an affirmative action program to demonstrate its commitment to equal opportunity employment. Further, Bess Goodman's performance may have an adverse effect on other managers and possibly on other employees.

At the end of the case, have the students consider the range of alternatives open to Grace Tyson. What should she do? How should she approach Bess Goodman? Should Grace Tyson force the issue, including getting higher management involved in this situation? Whatever she does, it is a difficult situation that must be handled firmly but with sensitivity.

CASE 45

AFFIRMATIVE ACTION AND WHOM TO HIRE

The following questions are intended to aid discussion pertaining to this case:

1. What is your evaluation of Ms. Triss? Is she qualified?
2. What is your evaluation of Mr. Young? Is he qualified?
3. Who is the most qualified?
4. Does the law require the hiring of unqualified applicants because of an affirmative action program? Of lesser-qualified applicants? Discuss.
5. Is there any wisdom in the advice of the company affirmative action office? If so, what?
6. Which applicant would you hire? Why?

This teaching note was prepared by Professor James C. Hodgetts of the Fogelman College of Business and Economics of Memphis State University as a basis for class discussion. Used by permission.

CASE 46

GENERAL PHYSICAL CONDITION AS AN OCCUPATIONAL QUALIFICATION

Although some students may believe that the questionable physical condition of applicant Jim Smith was the main reason for John Jones's reluctance to employ Smith, the main focus of this case involves the issue of age discrimination in the hiring decision. The case presents a good opportunity for reviewing the purpose of the Age Discrimination in Employment Act of 1967, as Amended in 1978 and 1984, the areas covered by the law, and the implications for private business. Considerations should cover economic, cultural-societal, and demographic perspectives. The case also can be used to explore how and why the law developed in the United States, whether or not it exists (at least in principle) in other countries, and why or why not.

DISCUSSION QUESTIONS

1. Given the apparently small size of John Jones's lumber yard, was his business covered by the act? Does it, or should it, make a difference in his hiring decisions?
2. How might John Jones have worded his advertisement differently in order to screen out more effectively what he considered to be unqualified applicants? Ask students to write new "Help Wanted" advertisements and compare responses.
3. How much weight should be given in Jones's hiring decision to current knowledge, experience, and physical condition? Discuss other pertinent considerations.
4. Given an average life expectancy of greater than 70 years, discuss the merits of Jones's "concern" in hiring Smith, an individual who is 45 years old.
5. There are some apparent inconsistencies in Jones's appraisal of just how much strenuous physical labor is involved in the job. Discuss the problems this may pose for Jones's response to the EEOC notice.
6. Jones has made a number of assumptions about the physical condition of applicant Jim Smith. How justified is Jones in making these judgments? How might Jones have approached his "concern" for Smith's physical condition differently (e.g., required medical examination prior to hiring, etc.)?
7. Did Jones, in fact, give Smith a reasonable opportunity to accept a position in the business? Discuss.

CASE 47

UNION INFLUENCE ON CONSTRUCTION COMPANY HIRING PRACTICES

This case vividly illustrates the "numbers game" problem that faces many employers who attempt to comply with the federal laws and regulations concerning nondiscrimination and affirmative action. It further illustrates the complicating influence of a labor organization, which also must be part of hiring practices, and decisions that comply with federal laws and that are also acceptable to the parties' labor agreements.

The following questions are suggested by the author of the case, Professor Kovach, to stimulate discussion.

DISCUSSION QUESTIONS

1. Are Brown Bros. in violation of federal fair employment practices?
2. To attain a more favorable racial balance, could Brown Bros. hire only nonwhite members of Local 444 as jobs in the company became available?
3. Could the union legally refer only nonwhite applicants to Brown Bros.?
4. What influences could be brought to bear on the Brotherhood of Electrical Workers to establish a more equitable distribution of nonwhite workers in the two locals?

FOREST PART CORPORATION: SELECTION AT ATTLEBORO

OBJECTIVE OF CASE

o To illustrate a staffing situation that involves dealing with
   organizational change and expose students to the mechanics of
   validating a selection device

KEY ISSUES

o Complexity of the validity process
o Decision making
o Human behavior
o Dealing with change

     The case attempts to provide the student with a realistic
view of one of the personnel function's major activities--staffing.
The problem of staffing is seen through the eyes of a personnel
director who learned on the job but has not kept up with his field.
In addition, the human resource demands must include affirmative
action considerations. Finally, data is provided from the files
of the personnel director. This data is to be used to determine
if the test for textile workers is valid.

DISCUSSION QUESTIONS

1. How justified do you believe Bob is in not worrying about the
    EEOC taking issue with the selection procedures for textile
    supervisors?

    Although the headquarters people seem to have taken a number of
    steps to develop a battery of valid and reliable instruments
    for their assessment center, they are not "home free." We are
    told the assessment center is "new," so we have no idea as to
    the center's effectiveness. In order to obtain this informa-
    tion, we might conduct an experiment that involves selecting
    people for supervisory positions. One group is chosen regard-
    less of assessment center performance (control group) and an
    equal number on the basis of their performance in the center.

     This teaching note was prepared by Professor George E. Stevens
of the College of Business Administration of the University of
Central Florida. Used by permission.

Performance and other ratings of effectiveness could be compiled for both groups after a specified time period.

2. Did Bob find a strong relationship between scores on the manual dexterity test and the number of units produced?

   The Spearman Rho (r_s) correlation for the whole sample is +0.40. This is not a significant correlation in this small a sample, but it is nevertheless strong enough to be suggestive that the test could be helpful.

3. Was there evidence of differential validity?

   There is evidence of differential validity.

Ethnic Origin	Age
W = + .75*; NW = + .40	< 30 = + .91*; > 30 = + .02

Marital Status	Education
S = + .59*; M = + .50	9-10 = + .47; 11-12 = + .56

   *Significant at the p < .05 level for a one-tailed test.

   As can be seen, the test score is strongly predictive of white job performance but only moderately predictive of nonwhite performance. When the age factor is considered, the test is strongly predictive for those under 30 years of age but does not predict performance for those 30 years of age and over. It is somewhat more predictive of nonmarried than married, but this tendency is slight. The test is somewhat more predictive of those with twelve or eleven years of education than those with ten or less years of education.

4. If you established a program for the textile workers, would you be able to use this test? If so, how would you use it?

   Given the differential validity results shown, the preliminary data indicates strong predictive validity for white but not nonwhite job performance. The test might be used for white textile workers only. Another test or selection measure must be found for nonwhites. Note: There is little difference in average production levels for the two groups. For whites, the average production level is 48.8 and for blacks it is 47.3. So all there is is a difference in the test's ability to predict performance, although the average production levels are comparable.

5. How thorough a job has Bob done in conducting his preliminary validation study?

   First, the size of the sample must be kept in mind. These results are, at best, indicative of a trend. One important issue is the comparability of the two samples drawn, those who were hired without regard for their test scores and those who

were hired on that basis. A second issue is that of possible
sex differences. All the workers in this sample are male.
Bob's rationale for not including women (aside from more work
being required) seems suspect.

CASE   49

HAZARD PROTECTION INSURANCE COMPANY

The clerical work measurement program at Hazard Protection Insurance Company was designed to give supervisors information by which to appraise progress of new employees in opening and processing incoming mail. Students may be surprised at the number of pieces of mail per day that can be opened and processed by an experienced employee. Nevertheless, these work standards seem to have been based upon observed performance of other employees, and a definite training time interval for reasonable work effectiveness has been developed.

It appears that Elaine Thompson, a young black employee, has not been able to progress as rapidly as other employees in the unit. It is not clear whether she is not capable of meeting the work standards, or whether she is spending too much time away from her job. Mary Matthews, her supervisor, feels that she cannot continue to ignore the situation, even though only three weeks of Elaine's training have elapsed. Ms. Matthew's apprehensions about handling the situation are in part related to the fact that she is white and Elaine Thompson is black, but should this really make any difference in this situation?

DISCUSSION QUESTIONS

1. Is it desirable to develop quantitative work standards for assessing the training progress of new employees? Why or why not?
2. Should a new employee be informed of the work standards that have been developed for a training period? (It is not clear whether Elaine Thompson was told what was expected of her.) Discuss.
3. Why is Mary Matthews concerned about how to handle this situation?
4. Evaluate the personnel director's statement to be "careful" in situations involving discipline of employees, particularly blacks.
5. Develop a course of action for Ms. Matthews to follow. Consider alternatives.

CASE 50

THE SEXIST REMARK

This short case incident will invoke considerable student discussion. Dr. Marshall considers his statement to be a sincere compliment; Ms. Cook calls it sexist. Who is right?

In recent years, feminists have been vocally critical of various language forms and stereotypes, which they feel consciously or unconsciously have discriminatory overtones. They have demanded that these be changed, and publishers in particular have been very sensitive to feminist complaints. (For example, the word chairperson is used instead of chairman; the words he or him are avoided as generic pronouns.) At the end of the case Dr. Marshall is disturbed about the implications of his "sexist remark," and he wonders about other language forms he customarily uses that may come under similar criticism.

DISCUSSION QUESTIONS

1. Was Ms. Cook's criticism of Dr. Marshall legitimate, or was it a put-down of the professor and in poor taste? Discuss.
2. Develop a list of words and/or stereotype language forms that conceivably might be considered sexist.
3. Are feminist efforts to change language patterns meaningful, or can such efforts cause unnecessary antagonism and become counterproductive? Discuss.

THE MIDVALE PLANT (B): THE RESIGNATION OF "MARY POPPINS"

This case presents a problem that is becoming more and more widespread in American industry as companies and other organizations seek to accelerate the advancement of minority employees. Some students will see this situation as an example of reverse discrimination. Maybe it is, and maybe it isn't. Regardless, several key members of Abacus's plant controller's office feel that a type of reverse discrimination is taking place. One employee, Mary Priesmeyer, nicknamed "Mary Poppins," has decided to leave; the promotion of a younger black woman is definitely a contributing factor to her decision. Another white male employee apparently is seriously considering leaving, since he feels that his sex and race are working against his opportunities at the Abacus plant.

The attitude of the older manager, George Whitfield, is also worth noting. Mr. Whitfield feels that the promotion of Gloria Hawkins is a direct result of the pressure the company is under to upgrade minority employees under an affirmative action program. This is a common belief held by many white employees, particularly white males. In Mr. Whitfield's case, his age may also be part of his apparent resentment concerning the promotion of Gloria Hawkins. The case offers a number of areas for discussion concerning this issue.

DISCUSSION QUESTIONS

1. Analyze the qualifications of Mary Priesmeyer as compared with the qualifications of Gloria Hawkins (from the information given in the case). Why is it difficult to ascertain whether Ms. Hawkins was promoted ahead of Ms. Priesmeyer because of her race?

2. To what degree should length of service play a role in promotions of this type? Discuss.

3. Analyze the qualifications of William Holt, who also is dissatisfied in this situation. Does he have a legitimate complaint concerning the promotion of Gloria Hawkins?

4. Many white males (like William Holt) feel that they have been victims of reverse discrimination in recent years. To what degree is this a legitimate complaint? How should a company answer this type of complaint to its white male employees?

5. At the end of the case, outline a course of action for Howard Howlett in regard to (a) how he should approach Gloria Hawkins about the problem; (b) how he should approach William Holt concerning his situation; and (c) how he should approach higher management in regard to the ramifications of this issue.

CASE 52

A PROBLEM OF TARDINESS

A common complaint among managers--which may in part be a
stereotype--is that a high percentage of blacks demonstrate
excessive tardiness and absenteeism on the job. Some black
employees have numerous difficulties, both real and imagined, in
getting to work on time, and George Douglas is certainly an
individual with more than his share of problems. As he is a
widower with six children, one can well imagine that it is most
difficult for him to be consistently punctual.

Douglas appears to be an excellent worker who has good in-
tentions. His willingness to make up lost time and to perform at
a superior pace are appreciated by his foreman, Lloyd Dauten. However, Dauten knows that he is under pressure from white employees
for "showing favoritism" to Douglas. In addition, Douglas's pere-
nial tardiness does create scheduling problems.

The latest incident described in the case is the straw that
may have broken the camel's back. Dauten knows that the situation
is getting out of hand, but he is perplexed as to how to deal with
it.

At the end of the case:

1. What alternatives are open to Dauten?
2. How should he approach George Douglas?
3. Is disciplinary action called for?
4. What should be Dauten's approach to the other workers in the
   department?
5. Outline a series of recommendations that Dauten might consider
   in dealing with this situation.

CASE 53

FREIDA MAE JONES

This case well illustrates the difficulties involved in managing and developing human resources when the backgrounds and experiences that individuals bring to a situation are so diverse. Career development efforts depend as much or more on the attitudes an individual demonstrates as on the value of the educational levels achieved and skills developed.

The reader of this case has an advantage in knowing something about the background and past experiences of Freida Mae Jones. Having that insight into her past perhaps makes it easier to understand and be empathic toward her. But some of this information probably is unknown to Mr. Luboda; and by the same token, Mr. Luboda, a white, middle-aged male shares a decidedly different interpretation of his behavior toward Ms. Jones. Luboda believes that he is being fair and equitable in the sense that he tries to spend time with all new employees, is willing and eager to help, and shapes the training experiences of each individual to complement the needs of his employees with the needs of his bank and its clients.

The instructor should certainly stress in this case that both individuals are viewing the situation from his/her own perspective without really making an effort to understand the issues from the other's point of view. This is not a situation of who is right and who is wrong. Rather, it vividly shows how perceptual differences develop and how they can seriously interfere with and impede cooperative and effective human resources management.

In examining Luboda's perspective, for example, it may be true that he holds misconceptions and stereotypes about women in professional roles, accounting for what Ms. Jones calls his over-cautious and prejudicial behavior. On the other hand, he may see Jones's sensitivity to the situation as a liability in nurturing the confidence he says is instrumental in gaining and keeping clients. For this reason, he prefers to accompany her to meetings to try to help her develop the skills she needs to establish rapport with customers. Each scenario is plausible, but which, if either, captures the real situation?

Further, it is not just the interests of Ms. Jones and Mr. Luboda that are important, but also the interests of the bank and the customers it serves. Can the conflicting points of view be reconciled to promote a stronger working relationship between

118

Jones and Luboda? It is not enough that a career training and
development program is in place. The individuals involved have to
make it work, and much of that effort means trying to understand
why each thinks and feels the way he/she does.

DISCUSSION QUESTIONS

1. Examine Jones's criticisms of Luboda. Is she being too
    sensitive? Is he overcompensating? Discuss the role that
    perception plays on interpretation of events.
2. Given the generally conservative nature of the banking
    business, does Luboda's responsibility as a manager justify
    his accompanying Jones to meetings with clients? Discuss.
3. What impact, positive or negative, might be created by Ms. Jones
    and the other black trainees spending so much time together
    during the program (both in terms of these trainees and the
    other participants)?
4. Examine Ms. Jones's comment that she feels she has to "fight
    all the time just to start off even" in light of her experiences
    in the training program and subsequent position in the branch
    office. Why does she feel that way?
5. Is the fact that Mr. Luboda treats Ms. Jones "differently" (if
    that is the case) an example of discriminatory treatment? Why
    or why not? Discuss the perception each individual brings to
    that interpretation of "different" treatment.

SAFETY FIRST (OR WHATEVER HAPPENED TO EQUAL OPPORTUNITY?)

RESEARCH BACKGROUND

Gopal Pati is a human relations/organizational development
consultant to Middle West Metal Fabricators, and Betty Anderson
came to him when the problem occurred. He already knew all the
participants in the drama, having worked with them for a number
of years in training and development, including equal employment
opportunity training sessions and management counseling, and he
talked with them about this problem while attempting to resolve it.

THE ISSUE

The primary concern in this case is how to implement equal
employment opportunity effectively. Most of the necessary ingredients of a successful program were already present at this
company: there was a strong, visible, and specific corporate
commitment to affirmative action and equal employment opportunity,
a good out-reach program, well-trained supervisors, and the presence of competent counselors. The authors feel that this organization is one of those rare manufacturing operations where
a supportive climate does exist in which human beings of all varie-
ties can survive, compete, and grow. Yet, in spite of this, some
male managers reverted to discriminatory behavior--perhaps inad-
vertently--while under pressure to get the product out, and others
let them get away with this behavior. Thus, the issue is primarily
one of control: standards for desired performance had been set,
but processes for comparing results against standards, and taking
corrective action, need to be present as well. And, as in most
control processes, most individuals met the standards without
intervention, but corrective measures needed to be present for
those few who did not.

In this particular case the equal employment training activities needed to be followed by extensive counseling and control for
those people who reverted to prejudicial behavior patterns when
back in the shop. Just as we have bench mark jobs, we need to

---

This teaching note was prepared by Professors Gopal C. Pati
and Darold Barnum of the Division of Business and Economics,
Indiana University Northwest. Used by permission.

identify bench mark people and to exercise especially careful
guidance and control over them on a continuous basis. Furthermore,
deep-rooted organizational reasons for such behavior need to be
understood and conditions modified on an ongoing basis to keep
them under control. If this is not done, this small number of
deviant individuals can completely undercut an organizational affirmative action plan and get the company into unproductive law-
suits. Moreover, vertical mobility for minorities and women will
continue to be the most-talked-about and least-done-about subject
of the decade.

INTERACTION: CASE AND COURSE DESIGN

The primary purpose of this case is to get students to realize
that merely talking about and setting goals and quotas is not
enough. It is also necessary to establish the procedures for
effectively implementing them and for controlling for deviance.
Although this may seem obvious, both authors have observed many
organizations, which, although they have comprehensive affirmative
action plans on paper, have had little success in practice for a
simple reason: lack of control and follow-up. Thus, this case
requires students to go beyond goal setting to design procedures
for goal implementation. The students must realize that in many
instances discrimination problems are really management problems
in disguise.

RELATING THE CASE

The students might be asked the following questions about the
case:

1. <u>What is management's objective?</u> To provide equal employment
   opportunity for all.

2. <u>What is the basic problem?</u> In some cases this company's Equal
   Employment Opportunity and Affirmative Action Program (EEO/AAP)
   objectives were not attained because of inadequate implementation and control procedures. This company had a congenial
   organizational climate and a comprehensive educational program.
   But here, as in most cases, there were a few individuals who
   would respond not to expectation but only to inspection. It
   is necessary that a system be present for monitoring and guiding these people. By "system" we don't mean creation of another bureaucratic structure to monitor the program. Control
   is an integral part of a manager's job.

3. <u>How should the problem be solved?</u> (a) Set up adequate control
   procedures. (b) Involve top line management of the organization in the effort. Staff involvement alone will not do the
   job, and it is important that line management be an active,
   not just a formal, part of the effort. (c) Use informal, as
   well as formal, means to communicate to the recidivists that
   biased behavior is not rewarded in the organization.

4. <u>What typical problems do women face when entering traditionally</u>
   <u>male jobs?</u>
   - Often a small group of vocal "male chauvinist pigs"
   - A lack of female peers to relate to; a scarcity of females
     with whom to discuss common problems, or who can serve as
     mentors
   - Need for a female to be "head and shoulders" above male
     counterparts to prove herself
   - Necessity to demonstrate assertiveness
   - Often, a few frustrated "dead enders" who resent and attempt
     to frustrate all other people's progress, but who use sex
     or race as an excuse for their behavior

5. <u>Do EEO/AAP training sessions alone result in equal opportunity?</u>
   No. If an organization sincerely wants to assimilate women
   into nontraditional jobs, it must improve its total organizational climate. Good personnel management in general is needed.

CASE   55

DISCHARGE DURING MATERNITY LEAVE

This case illustrates the dilemmas that employers face in trying to cope with employee discrimination charges even when the employer makes a good-faith effort to comply with applicable law.

The case of Polly Erwin vs. the Continental Mutual Insurance Company can be used for several purposes. First, it serves to introduce students to several bureaucratic forms and procedures of the Equal Employment Opportunity Commission.   Second, it focuses on sex discrimination due to pregnancy as covered by the Pregnancy Discrimination Act (which technically amended the Civil Rights Act of 1964).   Third, and probably most important, it forces students to apply their thinking concerning the specific issues involved and whether or not the employer did or did not violate the law in its actions in this case.

One way to approach the case is to have one or more students each research and prepare the case (a) from the position of Ms. Erwin and her attorney and (b) from the position of a company attorney. After each side has argued the case, the students in the class can then vote to decide whether or not the company was in violation of the law and whether or not Ms. Erwin was entitled to a cash settlement and reinstatement. (This might be conducted similar to an arbitration case simulation as described in this manual on pp. 8-9).

EPILOGUE

After the students have independently reached their conclusions concerning this case, the instructor may wish to provide the students with the actual outcome of the case.

In initial EEOC hearings, the company maintained that it had not violated any part of the applicable law, since the company felt it had treated Ms. Erwin no differently than it would treat any other employee's sickness or disability. But, Ms. Erwin maintained that the company should have accepted the pregnancy disability statements furnished by her midwife and doctor. She demanded reinstatement and appropriate back pay. The company refused and

_____

Note: All names and certain data—including on the EEOC "Settlement Agreement"—are disguised.

123

Mr. Richards indicated to EEOC that the company was prepared to litigate the matter through the federal courts, if necessary.

Subsequently, the company received a telephone call from EEOC reporting that Ms. Erwin had agreed to drop all discrimination and back pay settlement charges against the company if the company would give her her old job back. She had further indicated to EEOC that the man she was living with (that is, the father of her child, but not her husband) had left her, and she was now the sole support of the child.

After considerable debate, the company management agreed to reinstate Ms. Erwin rather than to face the extensive costs of possible litigation of the case in the courts. A copy of the settlement agreement follows, which the instructor may wish to reproduce for students.

Approximately one year after reinstatement, Mr. Richards described Ms. Erwin's situation to one of the case authors as follows: "At best, Polly is an average employee. She seems quite unhappy most of the time. I still wonder whether we made the right decision in reinstating her as we did."

Approximately two years after her reinstatement, Ms. Erwin was fired by the company for excessive absenteeism and poor work performance. Ms. Erwin did not contest her termination in any way.

EEOC SETTLEMENT AGREEMENT

In exchange for the promise made by <u>Continental Mutual Insurance Company</u> hereinafter referred to as the "respondent", contained in this Agreement, <u>Ms. Polly S. Erwin</u>, hereinafter referred to as the "person claiming to be aggrieved", agrees not to institute a lawsuit under Title VII of the Civil Rights Act of 1964, as amended, based on charge number <u>051792531</u> filed with the Equal Employment Opportunity Commission, and the Equal Employment Opportunity Commission agrees not to process the charge further.

It is understood that this agreement does not constitute an admission by the respondent of any violation of Title VII of the Civil Rights Act of 1964, as amended.

The respondent agrees to provide written notice to the Director of the St. Louis District Office within ten (10) days of satisfying each obligation contained in this agreement.

The person claiming to be aggrieved agrees to withdraw any charge(s) filed with a state or local fair employment agency covering the same matters alleged in the EEOC charge resolved by the present agreement.

The person claiming to be aggrieved and respondent agree that this agreement may be used as evidence in a subsequent proceeding in which any of the parties allege a breach of this agreement.

The Equal Employment Opportunity Commission's participation in this agreement does not reflect any judgment by the Commission on the merits of the charge. Furthermore, the Equal Employment Opportunity Commission does not waive its right to process any other charge, including a charge filed by a member of the Commission against the respondent.

In exchange for the promises of the person claiming to be aggrieved and the Equal Employment Opportunity Commission contained in this agreement, the respondent agrees

To reinstate person claiming to be aggrieved into position held

prior to maternity leave and at an hourly rate of $3.95 per hour.

To award person claiming to be aggrieved no loss of seniority

rights, opportunity for advancement or any other benefits or privi-

leges normally given to any other employee similarly situated.

Not to take any retaliatory action against person claiming to be

aggrieved because of the charge of discrimination filed against

Respondent.

DISCHARGE DURING MATERNITY LEAVE

Polly S. Erwin   *October 15, 1979*
Charging Party   Date

Lance R. Richards   *October 15, 1979*
Respondent   Date

APPROVED ON BEHALF OF THE COMMISSION

Sterling R. Cohen   *10-23-79*
District Director   Date

CASE 56

THE HANDICAPPED STUDENT AND THE REHABILITATION ACT OF 1973

This case can be useful for several purposes:

1. It introduces students to the Rehabilitation Act and its impli-
    cations for management decisions regarding handicapped people.
2. It raises pertinent questions concerning the meaning of "rea-
    sonable accommodations" for the handicapped, given other con-
    siderations such as costs, practicality, and the objectives to
    be accomplished.
3. It demonstrates the importance of sound planning and policies
    in this area, if approaches are to be developed that will be
    mutually satisfactory to all interests concerned.

At the end of the case, the "committee" has a number of alternatives open to it. Among the most likely are the following:

1. Hold the class in Waite Hall, using Professor White's "opera-
    tion chairlift" idea.
2. Move the class to Alexander Hall.
3. Juggle a number of other classroom assignments throughout the
    campus in order to make another suitable classroom available.

Each of these alternatives has pros and cons, which the students should be encouraged to discuss in depth before arriving at
their decision.

AUTHORS' NOTE

In the actual case situation, the committee decided to move
the class to Alexander Hall. Mr. Pyle was so notified, and he
accepted the decision accordingly. When a notice was posted in
Waite Hall concerning the room schedule change, no explanation was
given to the other students as to why the class had been moved to
the far east end of campus.

Professor White commented to one of the authors as follows:
"The classroom in Alexander Hall was barely satisfactory, but I
got by. Mr. Pyle got to class on his own in some way or other.
None of the other students said anything directly to me, but I
think that most of them understood why the class was moved out of
Waite Hall, and they accepted it without complaining--even though
it was quite inconvenient for them."

Dr. Jane Eason said as follows: "This case made me more aware of the necessity for us to know well in advance of the needs of all our handicapped people on campus. Since it's unlikely that the University will spend millions of dollars on its old buildings, we'll have to approach most of these problems on a case-by-case basis. We now have about fifteen severely handicapped students on campus. It's quite a major planning problem to accommodate all of them in ways that do not cause too much disruption elsewhere."

PART SIX

WAGE AND SALARY ADMINISTRATION

CASE 57

WHAT IS THE PROPER CHAUFFEUR'S RATE?

This case is designed primarily to stimulate discussion and thought on the problems of wage and salary administration. The instructor will find that it raises questions about general wage levels and policy, job evaluation, and wage payment methods.

A wage structure acceptable to company, union, and all the employees is an important but often difficult objective. This case illustrates the kind of problem that must be faced and re-solved in attaining such a wage structure and the fine line that divides the question of an internal wage structure from that of wage levels. Students are left to make their own rate award on the basis of the opposing arguments. The instructor may prefer to simulate this case in class using the arbitration case simula-tion approach described in this manual on pages 8-9.

In the actual case, the arbitrator carefully analyzed the positions of the parties. The following are brief excerpts from the arbitrator's decision, which the instructor may wish to share with students after they have first reached their own decision in the matter.

DECISION OF THE ARBITRATOR

> In the opinion of the Arbitrator, the arguments of each side present highly relevant factors, no one of which can be ignored in arriving at a determina-tion of what the wage rate should be for the classi-fication in question. Naturally, the problem is: What should be the relative weight given to each such factor? But before embarking upon a considera-tion of the latter question, the Arbitrator desires to state that he believes that there are additional factors which should be taken into consideration: the precise nature of the work and the number of em-ployees within the classification, the nature and size of the employer's business, the general posi-tion of the employee within the organization and the opportunities for advancement, the employee's relative freedom of movement or monotony of operation as the case may be.

The difference between $6.42 proposed by the
Company and the rates for drivers in various
other industries appears to be too great; that
difference averages well over a dollar or more.
This conclusion does not mean that the Arbitrator
believes that all drivers can be covered by one
comprehensive label--that of Truck Driver--and
emerge therefore with the same, or approximately
the same, wage rate. Wide differences in degrees
of job difficulty and individual skills required
are shown in the table of wage rates submitted by
the Union itself. But fully realizing that there
are truck divers and then there are other truck
drivers, a spread of a dollar between the rates
paid grocery drivers in the same metropolitan
area and the present chauffeurs who handle a 2 1/2
ton truck about the city streets is too large.

On the other hand, the Arbitrator believes that
the Company has established the validity of its
contention that something in the nature of a job
evaluation scheme, although not so labelled, has
been accepted and established by the practices of
the parties over a period of years. At all periods
pertinent to the discussion, the wage rates of
Stock Clerk and Shipping Clerk have been higher
than that of Chauffeur. The Company's evidence
that each of the former classifications requires
greater skill and entails greater responsibility
than does the latter was uncontradicted, as was its
evidence that in the past stock clerks and shipping
clerks had generally advanced to their respective
positions from prior employment as truck drivers.
Consequently, the experience of the Company and the
prior practices of the parties clearly show that in
any organizational table of skills and responsibilities,
the Chauffeur must be allocated a position somewhere
below the other two classifications.

The latter conclusion means that any rate set for
Chauffeur will necessarily have to be below the
generally prevailing rates for truck drivers in
other industries. In the opinion of the Arbitrator,
such a result is not inequitable to those presently
engaged as Chauffeurs. Since there is normally
only one regular full-time Chauffeur, it is obvious
that regard should be shown him more as a member
of the whole Sharon organization than as a truck
driver pure and simple. The history of the Company's
operations shows that, given efficient service in
his present employment, he has the prospect of
advancement to a more responsible position within
the organization. The relatively small size of the
Company makes the capacities of the individual employee more apparent to management and adds to the
personal touch. From the standpoint of the efficiency

of the Company's operations and the morale of employees, it would obviously be undesirable that
members of the organization, promoted to their
present positions from jobs as truck drivers,
should be outranked as to wages by a present truck
driver.

Conclusion

Accordingly, the latter conclusion, combined with
the prior finding that $6.42 per hour is too low,
requires that the rate for Chauffeur be set somewhere
between $6.42 and $6.82, the rate for Stock Clerk
under the new contract. The Arbitrator believes
that $6.62 per hour is a rate fair and equitable to
both parties. While it accords the Chauffeur a rate
about 20 cents per hour higher than the Company proposed, it maintains what the Arbitrator regards as a
necessary differential in favor of the Stock Clerk.

Award

The Arbitrator directs that the Wage Schedule of the
existent contract between the parties shall, insofar
as it affects the wage rate for the classification
of Chauffeur, read as follows in subsection (a):

(a) There is hereby established for the following job rates for the respective jobs
hereinafter set forth:

	From 1/1/77 thru 12/31/77	From 1/1/78 thru 12/31/78
Chauffeur	$6.62	$6.97

AUTHORS' NOTE

The above arbitration award has been disguised and modified
from the original case and wage data; but in other respects, the
arbitrator's award presented here is essentially as it was in the
real case situation. The instructor may wish to ask this question
of students: Was this a sound arbitration award, or was it just
a "split-the-difference" type of decision designed to offer a
partial "victory" to everyone?

CASE 58

THE STOW TRIBUNE COMPANY (B): THE CASE OF THE MISSING WORKER

OBJECTIVE OF CASE

o To illustrate a situation in which an organization's failure
   to do necessary contingency planning leaves the organization
   vulnerable if a key employee decides to depart

KEY ISSUES

o Organizational effectiveness
o Human resource utilization
o Compensation
o Training
o Performance evaluation

   The case illustrates a situation in which the department
manager has failed to evaluate the performance of his subordinates
and then proceeds to reprimand the wrong employee for failure
to perform. This manager also has not trained other employees in
two of the department's critical positions. These failures may
lead to expensive downtime.

DISCUSSION QUESTIONS

1. Should something be done about Terry Kinnear?

    A major part of the problem concerning Terry seems to be that
    he has developed into a very competent employee within a short
    period of time. The supervisor did not know how well he was
    performing and therefore has never rewarded him. The nature
    of Terry's job, particularly that of teletypesetter repairman,
    makes him extremely valuable to the organization. No one else
    is trained to maintain and repair these machines.

2. If you were Jim Godfrey, would you take any action? If so,
    what action would you take?

_____

    This teaching note was prepared by Professor George E. Stevens
of the College of Business Administration of the University of
Central Florida. Used by permission.

Jim's first act might be to swallow his pride and admit that he was wrong in reprimanding Terry. Mr. Godfrey handled the incident very badly. There is a need for him to get a better feel for how well his subordinates are performing.

3. Are there problems not directly related to the incident involving Terry Kinnear?

Yes. Basic issues that must be dealt with include the management style of Jim Godfrey, proper evaluation of the employee, assurance that compensation reflects the worth of his subordinates, and appropriate cross-training of subordinates so that all jobs may be covered at all times. At first blush, it may seem inappropriate to pay a less-tenured employee more or even the same amount as that paid to a more experienced employee. However, pay should include two components: merit and membership in the organization. Terry's ability to maintain the teletypesetters has saved the company a lot of money.

4. How would you rate Mike Pearson's handling of the affair?

Mike has left the problem in the hands of the manager. (Most managers would probably prefer not to have the personnel manager be more directive.) It is Mike's job to follow up this matter. Additionally, he can assist the manager in the area of performance evaluation and salary administration.

5. How would you rate Jim Godfrey's handling of the affair?

Jim did not handle the incident with Terry Kinnear very well. He jumped to conclusions about how much work Terry had done, then reprimanded him. Jim should have learned a lesson from the experience. In a union shop such an action might have led to the filing of a grievance. At best, bad feelings could have been caused. Jim's error was compounded by the fact that Jim left his workbench rather than face Terry when he returned.

CASE 59

CHARGES OF DISCRIMINATION AMONG THE LIBRARY STAFF

This case is an updated version of that which appeared in previous editions. However, only the dates and salary figures have been adjusted.

This case might well have been included in the equal employment opportunity section, because one of its major facets is a charge of racial discrimination. Since it also involves important issues of salary policy and salary administration, it has been included in the compensation section.

Several areas for discussion will present themselves. Among the items that the instructor should bring out in discussion are the following:

1. The question of merit in relationship to salary increase
2. Salary differentials between departmental working supervisors and rank-and-file employees
3. Confidentiality of wage and salary information
4. Salary rates and the question of discriminatory treatment

Students are likely to criticize the somewhat inept treatment of Carol Parker by library management at the campus library. The letter from the personnel director, Art Tipton, to Mrs. Parker seems to provide some justification for the salary situation. But one wonders whether Carol Parker will accept it as being an objective analysis, or whether she will consider it simply a rationalization to excuse the management for what she feels is racial discrimination.

The policy for employee grievances in a nonunion situation also will evoke some discussion. What should Mrs. Parker do if she feels that her problem has not been answered adequately?

Further, what should Art Tipton do to make sure that employee policies are followed and administered properly by line supervisors, particularly in view of the unionization threat?

JONES MANUFACTURING COMPANY

The first section involves a rather direct application of instructions in the text toward developing a numerical solution. Students' numerical answers to the problem will vary somewhat, depending upon the degree of accuracy they use in their calculations. However, their answers should come close to the solution presented here.

1. Tabular solution:

Job No.	Point Rating (X)	Hourly Rate (Y)	(X x Y)	(X^2)
1	275	$ 7.50	(2,062.50)	(75,625)
2	241	7.08	(1,706.28)	(58,081)
3	164	5.34	(875.76)	(26,896)
4	209	7.26	(1,517.34)	(43,681)
5	224	5.92	(1,326.08)	(50,176)
6	311	7.76	(2,413.36)	(96,721)
7	311	8.88	(2,761.68)	(96,721)
8	271	7.44	(2,016.24)	(73,441)
9	216	5.70	(1,231.20)	(46,656)
10	205	5.66	(1,160.30)	(42,025)
11	246	7.08	(1,741.68)	(60,516)
12	381	8.82	(3,360.40)	(145,161)
13	331	8.28	(2,740.68)	(109,561)
Totals (N = 13)	(3385) (ΣX)	(92.72) (ΣY)	(24,913.52) (ΣXY)	(925,261) (ΣX^2).

Equations (1) and (2) may be solved simultaneously by substituting the values from the table into these equations. Or, values for (a) and (b) in Equation (3) may be solved directly using the following formulas:

$$b = \frac{N(\Sigma XY) - (\Sigma X)(\Sigma Y)}{N(\Sigma X^2) - (\Sigma X)^2}$$

$$a = \overline{Y} - b\overline{X}$$

where $\overline{X}$ and $\overline{Y}$ are the mean values for X and Y, respectively.

Solving:

$$b = \frac{13(24,913.52) - (3385)(92.72)}{13(925,261) - (3385)^2} = .01757$$

$$a = 7.132 - (.01757)(260.38) = 2.5571$$

Equation (3) (rounded to facilitate calculations):

Hourly rate = 2.557 + (.01757)(Point value)

For 100 points: Hourly rate = 2.557 + 1.757 = 4.314

For 300 points: Hourly rate = 2.557 + 5.271 = 7.828

2. Tabular solution:

Grade	Point Range Minimum	Maximum	Hourly Rate Range Minimum	Maximum
10	162	183	$5.403	$5.772
9	184	205	5.790	6.159
8	206	227	6.176	6.545
7	228	249	6.563	6.932
6	250	271	6.950	7.318
5	272	293	7.336	7.705
4	294	315	7.723	8.092
3	316	337	8.109	8.478
2	338	359	8.496	8.865
1	360	381	8.882	9.251

3. Solving:

Upper Limit Rate = 1.10(a) + 1.10(b) Point value

= 1.10(2.557) + 1.10(.01757)(Point value)

Lower Limit Rate = .90(a) + .90(b) Point value

= .90(2.557) + .90(.01757)(Point value)

Substituting point values of 100 and 300 points in these two equations, the plots to draw the upper and lower limit lines are obtained, and the rectangles are constructed. See graphical solution.

4. Inspection will reveal that all jobs except Job #4 fall within the established rate ranges indicated by the rectangles. A number of other jobs, however, barely fall within the appropriate rectangles (for example, Jobs #7 and 10).

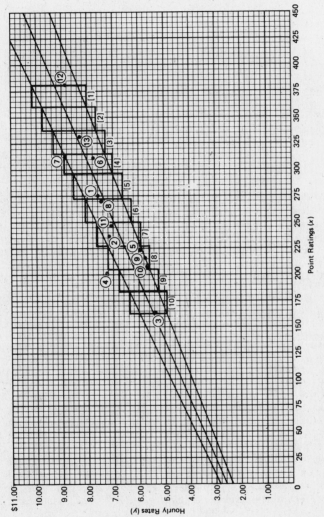

Circled Numbers Indicate Job Numbers
Bracketed Numbers Indicate Labor Grades

Tabular solution:

Job No.	Point Ratings	Present Actual Rate	Theoretically Correct Rate from Equation	Amount Difference (+) or (-)
1	275	$ 7.50	$ 7.389	- .111
2	241	7.08	6.791	- .289
3	164	5.34	5.438	+ .098
4	209	7.26	6.229	-1.031
5	224	5.92	6.493	+ .573
6	311	7.76	8.021	+ .261
7	311	8.88	8.021	- .859
8	271	7.44	7.318	- .122
9	216	5.70	6.352	+ .652
10	205	5.66	6.159	+ .499
11	246	7.08	6.879	- .201
12	381	8.82	9.251	+ .431
13	331	8.28	8.373	+ .093

5. Discussion of this item should suggest several alternatives open for handling of "red circle rates" (rates that lie completely outside of the rectangles). It should also suggest several policy alternatives for granting of wage increases to a person who may remain several years on the same job and therefore within the same labor grade (wage rate merit or seniority increases).

THE WAREHOUSE SITUATION

This situation illustrates that a job evaluation program can bring attention to additional problems and needs for adjustments. The warehouse department has some wage rates and point values clearly out of line with the data developed for the machine shop. For example, the lift truck operator's job is paid considerably higher than its point value assessment would indicate, whereas the loader's job is being paid too low in relation to its assessed point value.

What should be done to bring the ratings and hourly wages in the warehouse department into proper alignment? Here, as in the end of the first section of the case, numerous alternatives can be developed. Students should be cautioned in this situation, however, that the rates for the lift truck operators are going to be quite difficult to adjust. "Red circle jobs" on the scatter diagram (rates paid that are above or below the normal labor grade ranges) ordinarily need wage adjustments or changes in personnel.

CASE 61

THE TROUBLED BOOKKEEPING DEPARTMENT

This case has numerous facets for analysis, discussion, and recommendations. Problems within the bookkeeping department of the Apollo Excavating Company are evident in such areas as job performance, human relations, organization, and wage/salary administration.

The following case analysis and recommendations were developed by a student in a graduate case course in personnel/human resources management at Washington University. Although the authors do not necessarily concur with all of these ideas, they nevertheless should provide an instructor with fertile considerations for discussing the issues of and within the troubled bookkeeping department.

CASE ANALYSIS

First of all, there is a lack of communication between Coleman and Kelly. Kelly needs feedback on where she stands with management and what is specifically wrong with her performance. Coleman is informing her of day-to-day errors, but there is no effort to make a comprehensive evaluation. A formal employee evaluation system should be set up. Periodic evaluation interviews should inform employees of their strong as well as their weak points and stress how their strong points can help overcome problem areas. Interviews should be fair and objective evaluations of employee progress and include management assistance to help guide employees. Specific goals and objectives along with a time frame for accomplishing them should be discussed and agreed on during the interview. These objectives can then be used to measure employee performance at the next evaluation date.

As part of a formal evaluation system, an incident file to record especially good and bad employee performance should be maintained on each employee. This will document incidents and aid recall when evaluating employees. Specific employee actions will be much more meaningful than broad generalizations in substantiating evaluation interviews.

Research is needed to determine if wages paid by Apollo really reflect market wage rates. Using newspaper ads alone to determine wage rates may be inadequate. Federal surveys; construction surveys, including clerical employees; professional associations; and the local chamber of commerce would be additional places to check for information. An unrealistic view of market rates could be the reason that Apollo has not been able to attract good applicants. In any event, better information should be obtained to establish an accurate labor market picture.

Apollo's unwritten policy to raise employee salaries and provide the large bonuses each Christmas is not productive. It does not instill enthusiasm and, in fact, may accomplish the opposite. Because their salaries are raised each year regardless of performance, employees do not see a connection between job performance and pay rate increases. Therefore, employees have little real incentive to improve. Apollo needs to adopt a policy that increases employee wages by merit instead of seniority and "intimidation."

The transference of various duties among the office staff indicates analysis is required to determine new job descriptions. Job descriptions and local labor market rates can then be used to evaluate the monetary worth of the positions. Since Apollo's office staff is so small, a factor comparison method of evaluating should be sufficient.

Every effort should be made to bring wages into line with the new job evaluations, increase communication, dispense with large bonuses, and provide employee evaluations (reinforced by incident files). In view of Apollo's past inability to attract ample qualified job applicants, Apollo should continue to pay the high wages in the labor market. This may help to persuade good applicants to work for a firm with fewer advancement opportunities. Private employment agencies may be a better alternative to newspaper ads in soliciting job applicants. A good agency could test and screen individuals and provide a pool of applicants to choose from.

Coleman should sit down with Lila Kelly immediately and discuss his dissatisfaction:

1. He should be candid and specific as to what the problems have been in the past as well as reinforce any strengths she may have.
2. Kelly should be made to see the importance of her job, and hopefully pride will motivate her to improve her work performance.
3. Together they should set specific goals to be achieved within a reasonable time and schedule a date to re-evaluate her performance.
4. Coleman should let Kelly know he is there to help her achieve success, but that she must do her part and perform up to expectations.
5. Supervision of Mae Parton and responsibility for the bookkeeping department should be given back to Kelly. Kelly should be held accountable for this responsibility as one of her objectives.
6. Since Kelly has access to all payroll information, Coleman should explain the monetary adjustments to be made based on the new job evaluations, especially if David Hayes is to receive

a larger amount than she. The explanation should include how
the jobs were evaluated, how the duties of her position have
been changed as compared with those of the previous supervisor,
and what expertise is required in Hayes's position. Coleman
should listen to any reasonable objections and correct any
oversights he may have made.

A new wage policy (without automatic bonuses) should be written
and communicated to employees so that they will know better what
to expect in the future. All raises should be administered as
indicated by the new job evaluations and in accordance with the
guidelines to be set in the wage policy.

In summary, Coleman should try to help Kelly through better
communication and feedback on her work; but basically she needs
to perform, be terminated, or transferred to her old position if
it becomes vacant. If termination does occur, the accounting firm
will be there to direct and guide the bookkeeping department until
a replacement is hired.

CASE 62

PETRI CHEMICAL COMPANY (C):   TOM MOXLEY

This case illustrates problems of wage and salary administration and how they are related to such factors as employee appraisal, supervisory technique, and employee motivation.

The wage data in this case have been updated from previous editions of the text.   However, the basic problem in the case remains the same.

It appears that the Petri Company is handling Tom Moxley in an individual context, rather than on an overall policy basis.   If the company goes too far in trying to pacify Tom Moxley, there may arise more serious issues of dealing with similar complaints by other employees both outside and within the union situation.

DISCUSSION QUESTIONS

1.   Evaluate the salary policies with respect to laboratory technicians.
2.   Were Tom Moxley's complaints warranted?   Why or why not?
3.   Why was Moxley placing his supervisor under so much pressure regarding his salary?
4.   Evaluate the solution offered by the superintendent at the end of the case.

An interesting exercise is to have students assume that they have been hired as consultants to the Petri Chemical Company on wage policy.   What changes in wage and salary administration could be suggested?

CASE 63

THE ENGINEERING DEPARTMENT SALARY ADMINISTRATION PLAN

Probably the major value of this case lies in its description of a plan to compensate professional employees, in this case, engineers. The problem of developing rational and fair bases for compensation of technical, clerical, professional, and other types of white-collar workers is one that is difficult for most companies.

An interesting aspect of the plan at Majestic Corporation is its attempt to tie together into one basic plan such factors as performance, job grades, raise money available, raise frequency, and promotional policy. The major "hang-up" seems to occur in the administration of the plan, where the "potential for promotion" ratings somehow enter into the thinking of the managers and salary administrators.

It is understandable why the company may want to push its younger engineers' salaries along faster, since this may be necessary to both attract and retain younger professional people. On the other hand, this creates the serious problem of equity with older engineers, who have performed well for many years but whose potential for growth in the company is no longer promising.

At the end of the case, Green and Benson are pondering what they should do in order to implement better the current salary plan and suggest changes in the overall salary administration policy for their department. Have students place themselves in the situation of Green and Benson and outline recommended courses of action.

CASE 64

OLD WORLD DELI: TIPS AND THE WAGE/HOUR LAW

As background information to this case, the following excerpts
from the publication, "Handy Reference Guide to the Fair Labor
Standards Act" published by the U.S. Department of Labor in 1977
may be helpful to instructors.

The Fair Labor Standards Act establishes
minimum wage, overtime pay, equal pay,
recordkeeping, and child labor standards
affecting more than 50 million full-time
and part-time workers.

BASIC WAGE STANDARDS

Covered non-exempt workers are entitled to a minimum
wage of not less than

Beginning January 1, 1978 -- $2.65 an hour
Beginning January 1, 1979 -- $2.90 an hour
Beginning January 1, 1980 -- $3.10 an hour
Beginning January 1, 1981 -- $3.35 an hour

AND

OVERTIME AT NOT LESS THAN
ONE AND ONE-HALF TIMES THE EMPLOYEE'S
REGULAR RATE IS DUE AFTER 40 HOURS OF
WORK IN THE WORKWEEK

WAGES WHICH ARE REQUIRED BY THE ACT ARE DUE ON THE REGULAR
PAY DAY FOR THE PAY PERIOD COVERED

TIPPED EMPLOYEES

Tipped employees are those who customarily and regularly receive more than $30 a month in tips. The
employer may consider tips as part of wages, but such
a wage credit must not exceed 50 percent of the minimum
wage (beginning January 1, 1979, 45% is the maximum

tip credit, and beginning January 1, 1980, 40% is
the maximum tip credit).

The employer who elects to use the tip credit pro-
vision must inform the employee in advance and must
be able to show that the employee receives at least
the minimum wage when direct wages and the tip credit
allowance are combined. Also, employees must retain
all of their tips, except to the extent that they
participate in a valid tip pooling or sharing arrangement.

RECORDKEEPING

Employers are required to keep records on wages,
hours and other items, as specified in the Division's
recordkeeping regulations. Most of the information
is of the kind generally maintained by employers in
ordinary business practice and in compliance with
other laws and regulations. The records do not have
to be kept in any particular form and time clocks
need not be used. With respect to an employee subject
to both minimum wage and overtime pay provisions, the
following records must be kept:

- Personal information, including employee's name,
  home address, occupation, sex, and birth date (if
  under 19 years of age)
- Hour and day when workweek begins
- Total hours worked each workday and each workweek
- Total daily or weekly straight-time earnings
- Regular hourly pay rate for any week when overtime
  is worked
- Total overtime pay for the workweek
- Deductions from or additions to wages
- Total wages paid each pay period
- Date of payment and pay period covered

Instructors are cautioned that the above provisions were in
place at the time of publication of the text, and that these provisions may have been amended by Congress subsequently. Also,
instructors may wish to familiarize themselves with more of the
details of Fair Labor Standards Act, as amended, particularly in
regard to enforcement policies and procedures of the Wage/Hour
Division of the Department of Labor.

As the law pertains to the Old World Deli case, it is clear
that Ken Feldor has been rather loose and indifferent in his approach to the reporting of tips by his waitresses. Both Ken Feldor
and the parent company's vice president for operations, Randy
Norman, seem to be taking a "there's not much we can do" approach
to this situation. Yet, the problems raised in their interview
with Betty Atkins must not be shrugged off. These problems are

serious from a legal standpoint as well as from a human resources management point of view. The questions suggested below should provide avenues for both problem analysis and suggested solutions.

DISCUSSION QUESTIONS

1. Discuss the complaint of the employees concerning the music and dress code at Old World Deli & Cafe. Are these complaints to be taken seriously, or discounted as being little more than typical griping?
2. Why is the reporting of tips by waitresses a major source of both employee and management irritation?
3. If the Wage/Hour Division of the U.S. Department of Labor investigates the Old World Deli & Cafe, can management be held liable for any inaccurate reporting of tips? (Suggestion: Have a student call or visit the nearest regional office of the Wage/Hour Division to ask how this type of problem is investigated and what remedies are usually implemented.)
4. Are the amount of tips a good measure of waitress productivity? Why or why not? Would a formal performance appraisal system be desirable? Discuss.
5. Outline a series of steps that you would recommend to Ken Feldor to deal with the problems identified in this case.
6. Refer to Footnote 2 at the end of the case. Do you believe that this approach has encouraged more honest reporting of tipped income? Why or why not? (Suggestion: Have a student call or visit a regional office of the Internal Revenue Service for their opinion and additional information.)

CASE 65

NOVAC COMPANY

This case has been updated somewhat from the version presented in previous editions of the text. Certain wage data have been adjusted to approximate more recent levels, but in other respects, the case is identical to the case originally written by Professor Cronin.

Wage payment on the basis of output (wage incentives) generally is considered appropriate when: (1) the units of output are measurable; (2) a clear relation can be found between employee effort and the amount of output; (3) jobs are standardized and work flows are consistent; and (4) quality considerations are less important than the quantity of output desired. A close examination of this case reveals that all of these criteria are not met by conditions in the Novac Company.

From the data available, a wage incentive plan, if implemented, probably would apply to some 250 workers. What would this mean for the other some 450 employees who are doing staff and indirect labor? (For an illustration of the types of problems that might arise, see the Filmore Electric Co. (B) case, Case 72.)

If the assembly department is only 60 to 70 percent efficient, would an incentive plan cure the inefficiency? Is it possible that poor supervision is responsible for the lack of efficiency in assembling? Further, the multitude of suggestions received in the suggestion program would indicate that many areas of savings still could be explored.

There is also the matter of costs. Will the cost savings expected to be realized from increased productivity under the wage incentive program compensate for the additional cost to set up and administer the incentive system? What will be the effect of the wage incentive system on the employment problem? Will it help attract workers to Novac, or will it do the reverse?

Have the students analyze this case as if they were a management consulting firm brought in to analyze all data and the problems presented in the case at the Novac Company. Have them outline a plan or a series of recommendations to the company.

CASE 66

THE SUPERINTENDENT'S VACATION PAY

This case illustrates several problems in connection with salary and wage administration. It also gives insight into changing attitudes toward wage supplements. The salary figure in the case has been adjusted upward to reflect more recent levels. Otherwise, the case is identical to that which appeared in previous editions of the book.

DISCUSSION QUESTIONS

1. Should the school board have developed a policy with respect to the payment of a vacation allowance to employees who leave the system without having used their accumulated vacation?
2. Does it make any difference that the "employee" in this case receives $42,000 per year?
3. Does it make any difference that his contract had not expired?
4. Are vacations a reward for past service, a time to rest in anticipation of another year's work, or merely a part of an employee's compensation?

CASE 67

AVERY DRUG COMPANY: DON MORAN

This case can be used for a number of purposes. First of all, it demonstrates a compensation plan for salespeople and the problems attendant to a salary-plus-bonus plan. More important, however, is the problem of changing from an incentive-type plan to one based on straight salary and how to communicate such a major change in salary policy.

On the basis of the figures presented in the case, it would appear that Don Moran has been treated fairly by Division Manager Hank Logan in his change to a straight salary status. However, Don Moran apparently believes that he has been unfairly treated, and his telegram to Logan indicates that he is quite dissatisfied with his new salary. Some of Don Moran's disappointment may be related to poor communication. On the other hand, it may be related to a feeling that he was being rewarded more fairly on an incentive type of plan. Perhaps he feels that he was a good producer and that other sales people are not doing their share. Under a straight salary basis, will there be a loss of incentive by salespeople to put forth superior effort?

At the end of the case, the student is probably just as confused as Division Manager Hank Logan. Certainly, there is a need for Logan and Moran to sit down together and talk about this situation. A good way to handle the case would be to have the students prepare a list of specific questions that Logan should be asking Moran, as well as what areas of information Logan should be prepared to give Moran when they get together to discuss his salary situation. A role play of this meeting is a desirable way to bring out feelings and issues involved in this case situation.

CASE 68

SALARY DISCRIMINATION AT ACME MANUFACTURING

This case illustrates the problems presented in an employment situation that lacks a credible job evaluation system. There is little evidence of any systematic approach to setting salary levels. The personnel director has only vague suppositions about how previous salary decisions were made.

It appears that at least part of the historical approach for determination of salaries involved a rating of the persons and not the jobs. Job evaluations must be objective and not biased by personal feelings about an individual in a position, that is, someone who may be either overqualified or underqualified for the job.

Over 50 percent of the salaried employees are female, and yet only 4 of these 14 salaried women are in management positions. From an equal employment opportunity perspective, this may in itself be a problem. Further, Joe Blackenship is properly concerned that the women in management positions are not being paid the same as the male supervisors. Since there are not any similar supervisory jobs currently occupied by both men and women, the issue of equal pay for equal work previously has not been addressed. And yet this is just what a good job evaluation could provide. Job evaluation seeks to identify the degrees of skill, effort, and responsibility in each position, along with the relative money value associated with each job. When a job evaluation is performed, Blackenship's concerns are realized. The question now becomes how to rectify the inequities.

A good instructional approach is to take a class poll to see how the students are divided among the four alternatives Blackenship has identified. Have students justify their positions.

DISCUSSION QUESTIONS

1. Discuss Joe Blackenship's decision to hire a compensation consultant rather than his taking the time to utilize the expertise he had with a previous job evaluation system.
2. A modified ranking method of job evaluation was chosen. What other methods might have been implemented? Discuss the pros and cons of the ranking method in this particular situation.

3. Evaluate Blackenship's offer of a sizable salary increase to the personnel director. Has he "solved" this problem? Consider the equity issue in relation to the three supervisors who have also been underpaid.
4. Should any company "good will" considerations influence the choice among the four alternatives? Why or why not?
5. From an economic standpoint, would the company be justified in choosing an alternative that is the least expensive? What about from an ethical perspective? A social responsibility perspective? A legal perspective?

PART SEVEN

EMPLOYEE REPRESENTATION:
THE ROLE OF THE LABOR UNION

ON ORGANIZING A LABOR UNION: AN INTERVIEW WITH A UNION OFFICIAL

This interview-type case can be used to illustrate a number of basic points in regard to union-management relationships. It focuses primarily on the matter of the initial organization of a labor union, but the message goes far beyond this--to the total process of human resource management.

Probably the most telling indictment that the union official makes is that the best organizers are not on the union payroll. He says, "Unions just don't happen in a plant; they're caused. And it's management, not the unions, that causes them." There is probably considerable truth in what he says. If management has not provided its employees with the kind of employment atmosphere the employees want or expect, the union organizer has a considerable opportunity to convince employees that they need a union.

The tactics used by a typical union organizer are rather interesting to discuss. But more importantly, the union official points out that the inept reactions of management often play directly into the hands of the union organizer.

The issue of organizing "to reach a balance," as stated by the union official, is also important to bring out in this case. Many employers believe that they should have complete and virtually unquestioned authority over employees. Small businesspeople, according to the union official, tend to feel this way. It should be self-evident that current personnel philosophy and reality suggest that this type of management attitude is long out-of-date. Unless managers in nonunion organizations learn how to meet the total expectations of their employees, they are prime candidates for the labor organizer.

CASE 70

McGRATH HOSPITAL

The McGrath Hospital case will offer students a good example
of how a personnel director or any manager should not deal with a
union organizing campaign. Pete Watson, apparently unfamiliar and
unaccustomed to any type of union efforts in his hospital, is reacting, rather than having a sound strategy for meeting the union's
organization attempt.

Union organizers have a legal right to distribute literature
outside of the premises of a company or hospital they are trying
to organize. The fact that a number of employees at McGrath Hospital are complaining to management about being "bothered" by union
organizers should be approached by management cautiously and sensi-
tively. However, Personnel Director Pete Watson reacts with a very
strongly worded letter that could backfire on him by mobilizing
sentiments of employees to be sympathetic to union organizers. In
his letter Watson tells employees to contact their supervisors for
answers to questions. There is no evidence in the case that the
supervisors would know how to respond to any questions the employees might have.

The union committee members are angry, perhaps justifiably so.
The long-service employees feel that Watson's letter was quite unfair in labeling them as "strangers." At the end of the case, the
union organizing committee and their local union president, Mr.
Brown, are to discuss the situation with Mr. Watson. However, Mr.
Watson is reluctant to meet with Mr. Brown as part of the committee
meeting. Here, too, Mr. Watson is on dangerous grounds, politically
as well as legally. It appears that Mr. Watson is again reacting,
rather than thinking calmly about how he can meet the union challenge positively.

DISCUSSION QUESTIONS

1. What should have been the hospital management's response to the
    employees' complaints that they were being bothered with con-
    gestion around the main entrance due to union organizers? Is
    a policy needed for this issue?

2. Analyze how Mr. Watson might have written a letter in non-
    inflammatory terms. Develop a letter that would express the
    hospital's point of view without antagonizing various indi-
    viduals.

158

3. Is Mr. Watson obligated to meet with the union organizing committee, including the local union president, Mr. Brown? Is the answer to this a legal or a diplomatic one? Discuss.

4. At the end of the case, develop a strategy for the hospital to use in approaching the union organizing campaign.

CASE 71

MANAGEMENT PERSUASION OF POTENTIAL UNION MEMBERS

The case introduces a number of issues, but perhaps what it illustrates best is the impact that Wesley Hall's management style and attitude toward unions have on organizational performance.

There are two major problem areas. First, in his position as president of the company, Wesley Hall's admonition to his supervisors to squash any union organizational effort sets a precedent for similar behavior patterns among other members of management. Hall's style of circumventing the real issues by resorting to questionable tactics is imitated in the behavior of Art Jones, which demonstrates the impact that management style can have on an organization.

Second, Art Jones's unusual effort to hire the only qualified applicant he has seen compromises the company's legal position. His deal with Bill Swigart is an example of what has long been illegal; it presents the instructor an opportunity to review the so-called "yellow dog contract" (in this case, without the actual written contract). In addition, Jones's offer of a higher wage in exchange for Swigart's agreement to refrain from union activities is blatant interference and could certainly generate NLRB charges against the company.

The list goes on. The discussion questions highlight some additional issues.

DISCUSSION QUESTIONS

1. Discuss the impact that rumors can have on organizational communication patterns. Does the informal network have a legitimate place in the work environment? How else might Hall have responded to the rumors?
2. Is Wesley Hall's request that Art Jones hire a new machine operator "with no prior record of union membership" legal? At what point does it transcend that legal boundary?
3. Discuss Hall's attitude and approach toward union affiliation. (This presents an opportunity to refer to Case 69, "On Organizing a Labor Union.") What are the potential ramifications?
4. Identify the flaws in Art Jones's tactics. What led him to resort to such measures (i.e., lack of professional training, ignorance of labor law, leadership influences, etc.)?

160

5. Did Jones have the authority, either explicit or implied, to hire Swigart at a higher salary level? Discuss.
6. Is Bill Swigart bound by his word to Jones to refrain from union activities? What legal steps are afforded to him at this point, based on the company's actions?
7. How would the NLRB be likely to rule on the various actions taken at Cahen Mills? Discuss possible remedies.

CASE 72

FILMORE ELECTRIC COMPANY (B): THE ASSEMBLY DEPARTMENT

Labor union leaders are the first to say that management is often their best ally when it comes to organizing a plant or work group. This implies that either because of management's actions or lack of actions, workers will turn to a labor union in order to seek relief from real or imagined grievances and problems. This makes a labor union's organizing efforts that much easier.

In this case, there is just such a situation. Management, principally in the person of an industrial engineer, John Bosch, has instituted a wage incentive system in a departmental situation that is hardly conducive to it. In fact, the wage incentive plan has accomplished little except to aggravate an already status-strained relationship between the line Section A and the assemblers in Sections B and C. The union proponents within the department have capitalized on the friction as a major selling point in trying to sign up members for the union. Yet John Bosch states, in an almost cavalier fashion, that the union situation is not his concern.

The departmental foreman, Henry Freitel, also displays a rather indifferent attitude toward the union organizing efforts, even though he is aware that top management is against the idea of a union entering the plant. There is no indication in the case that top management is aware of the situation in the assembly department. Freitel states that he is in a virtually helpless position; yet has he sought assistance from top management in trying to respond to the tactics of the union in his department?

Unless something is done soon to counter the union appeal, the assembly department will probably be organized in the near future. If Freitel's estimate is correct, nearly half of the department's personnel already have signed union cards; a few more pledges will give the union enough members to carry an NLRB representational election.

Is it too late? As a class exercise, assume that top management becomes aware of the situation. What courses of action would you recommend to management to counter the organizing efforts of the union (within legal limitations, of course)?

162

FILMORE ELECTRIC COMPANY (C):
COMMUNICATIONS DURING A UNION ORGANIZATIONAL CAMPAIGN

This case is the follow-up case to case 72. It contains two letters sent by the company and two sent by the labor union to employees during the course of the organizing campaign.

The case can be used first of all to illustrate the types of arguments typically presented by management to counter a union campaign. Mr. Filmore, company president, has carefully worded his letters to stay within compliance of all labor laws and at the same time to get across management's point of view. Noticeably, however, Mr. Filmore speaks in generalities and is not very specific concerning some of the issues brought forth by the union.

The union letters are similarly broadly stated, although there is a noticeable specificity aimed at the questions of piece rates set by time-study men in the company. The union letters can be related directly to the problems apparent in the Filmore Electric (B) case, where the time-study rates are a major part of growing dissatisfaction.

After discussion of these letters in relationship to case 72, it is probably appropriate to inform the students that the employees of the Filmore Company voted approximately 2 to 1 in favor of affiliating with the International Electrical Workers Union. The discussion can then focus on how the union capitalized on various areas of dissatisfaction and on management's relative indifference to the situation as shown in the assembly department case. Apparently, the sentiments of the workers were mobilized by what went on in the plant, and Mr. Filmore's letters to the employees were not sufficient to overcome the message that the union organizers gave to the workers.

This case might also be related to case 69, "On Organizing a Labor Union." Here a labor official stated that the best union organizers are management itself and the things that management does or fails to do. The Filmore Electric Company gives a vivid example of what this labor official was talking about.

CASE 74

FILMORE ELECTRIC COMPANY (D): UNION-MANAGEMENT RELATIONSHIPS

The Filmore Electric Company (D) case obviously removes any doubt as to the outcome of the union organizational campaign that was described in Cases 72 and 73. The union won a resounding victory--actually the vote was about 2 to 1 in favor of the union--to gain representational rights for employees in a number of production departments at the Filmore Company. The Filmore (D) case presents insights into the early encounters between representatives from both sides and how these reflect both personal as well as institutional considerations that will be crucial in the developing relationships between the parties.

It is apparent that the union business agent, Bill Riley, is determined to establish himself as a formidable opponent early in the negotiations. It is equally apparent that the personnel director, Steve Blumenkamp, understands that personal abuse is not necessary, and he refuses to accept it in the first meeting described in the case.

Most of the case thereafter involves the subsequent meeting between Riley and Blumenkamp in which they discuss their backgrounds and certain bargaining issues. This type of frank discussion can do much to help both sides better understand where the other "is coming from" and can facilitate in moving the union-management relationships from one of considerable acrimony and tension to one in which constructive problem solving can be achieved.

The problem of the incentive rates and the company's so-called merit rating system tied to performance and production will be major sticking points between the parties. The instructor should refer back to Cases 72 and 73 for reference to the problems inherent in these plans, and the following questions should generate considerable discussion concerning where union/management relationships at the Filmore Company are likely to be headed.

DISCUSSION QUESTIONS

1. Was Steve Blumenkamp well advised for excusing himself from the meeting when the union business representative, Bill Riley, used abusive language about him? Why or why not?
2. Evaluate the personal backgrounds of Blumenkamp and Riley. Will these be helpful or detrimental to building relationships between the parties? Discuss.

164

3. Discuss Bill Riley's reasons for opposing the company's merit (performance) rating plan. Include in this discussion Riley's political position as a union leader.
4. Discuss Blumenkamp's reasons for wanting to have a performance rating/bonus program. Is the evaluation form (Exhibit 74-1) appropriate for the types of jobs in the company?
5. Evaluate the conversation between Blumenkamp and Riley concerning how the union chooses its shop stewards. Why is this an important aspect of ongoing union-management relationships?

EPILOGUE

After thoroughly discussing this case, the instructor may wish to inform the students that the so-called performance or merit rating plan for the hourly-paid union employees continued to generate numerous union objections and a number of union grievances. Not only did the union continue to protest, but the plant supervisors also complained to upper management that it was causing more harm than good. About ten months after the union became the official bargaining representative for the plant employees, the company decided to end the plant merit rating plan and agreed to hourly negotiated wage rates for plant employees as advocated by the union. Only supervisory, clerical, and salaried (i.e., nonunion) personnel remained under a merit rating system.

CASE 75

OLYMPIC CORPORATION

    This case will provide a fascinating discussion of many facets
of union-management relationships. First of all, students will be
forced to speculate about the reasons for the deterioration in
union and management relationships at Plant 37. Dan Maurice, the
union president, appears to be under pressure from his members to
be more militant in dealings with management, but one wonders whether or not management, too, has contributed in part to his actions
in the first part of the case.

    The work stoppage that takes place in the press department is
a culmination of the serious deterioration in union-management relationships. It is apparent that the work stoppage has been planned
by someone, with the quite evident likelihood of Mr. Maurice's
involvement. However, the instructor should point out to the
students that management has no proof of Maurice's actual direction
of the work stoppage.

    At the end of the work stoppage incident, management is con-
fronted with a critical point of decision. Legally, the company
could discipline all of the workers involved in the stoppage.
What would be the advantages of choosing this course of action?
What would be the dangers of this type of drastic action?

    Management reaches a decision to suspend the three union offi-
cers most directly involved in the work stoppage. It should be
pointed out to students that, technically, this decision would be
upheld in most situations by labor arbitrators, since arbitrators
have generally held that union leaders must bear responsibility
for the actions of their workers in wildcat work stoppages. However, the response of the union membership to the suspension action
was quick in coming, a vivid illustration of solidarity of union
members when their leaders are threatened or punished by stern
actions of management.

    The actions of Mr. Palmer subsequent to the walkout are in-
deed interesting. From a posture of firmness, in which he insists
on no negotiations until workers are back on their jobs, Mr. Palmer
suddenly changes in the hearing meeting of Thursday, October 12.
In this meeting, it is apparent that the union leaders involved
are not about to admit guilt in this matter, even though their
positions are weak in regard to their members' actions. Yet Mr.
Palmer suddenly backs down and decides to reduce the degree of
discipline of the union leaders in return for a rather loosely

166

worded promise and to avoid the filing of a grievance. At this
point, Mr. Palmer has changed his position from a strong one to a
conciliatory one, and students should recognize what this may cost
him in terms of the respect union officers will have for him in
the future.

Mr. Palmer's letter to the members of the local will also
evoke a certain amount of discussion. Mr. Palmer hopes that this
letter will have some positive effect, but one can speculate about
whether the letter will influence members to turn from their leaders in the event of another dispute of this kind.

Mr. Maurice's return to the job and the suspension of two
union shop stewards are accompanied by an apparent slowdown in
operations. Here, too, management appears rather helpless in com-
bating this type of informally arranged defiance of management
objectives. This illustrates that the real source of management
leadership is often found in the degree of "followership" that the
workers are willing to express. In the presence of a strong, militant labor union, management may find its leadership efforts ham-
pered because of the dual allegiance held by the workers toward
company and union.

In the past, instructors at Washington University have used a
role-play situation at the end of the case. This role play has
four students simulate the Wednesday morning meeting of Mr. Palmer
and his staff. These role plays will force students to bring out
rather strong positions regarding labor unions. Most students--
most people for that matter--are either for or against labor unions,
and the role plays attempt to force the students to take strong
positions in the Wednesday morning simulated meeting. Usually,
the effect of these strong positions will be a serious obstacle
to the meeting's establishing a sound procedure to attempt to cope
with the situation. This can be pointed out by the instructor at
the end of the meeting; usually the instructor will be forced to
terminate the meeting after some ten or fifteen minutes of role
play.

The role plays for each of the four individuals involved are
as follows:

ROLE FOR ROBERT PALMER

As plant manager, you are interested primarily in one thing:
improving plant performance. You felt that relations with the
union had been satisfactory prior to the walkout, and that relations will be better in the future if management forces will try
to be a bit more cordial to union leaders than they have been in
the past. At the moment, you are under heavy pressure from top
company officials to get the plant performance straightened out,
and you feel that management in the plant will have to "give" something to the union in order to get better production and efficiency.

OLYMPIC CORPORATION

Play this role in the Wednesday morning meeting. You are
free to try anything that will fit within the general context of
this role.

ROLE FOR TOM HARPER

As personnel supervisor, you feel that the time has come for
plant management to take a strong stand. You advocated trying to
fire the union president in connection with the plant walkout, but
you were overruled by Mr. Palmer, who feared another stoppage.

Your personal beliefs are strongly antiunion. In your opinion,
unions are virtually in league with the devil, communists, and other
sinister forces. You advocate a strong management position in all
dealings with the union, particularly with Mr. Maurice.

Play this role in the Wednesday morning meeting. You are free
to say anything and advocate any solution to the plant problem that
will fit within the general context of this role.

ROLE FOR ART GAEBLER

As assistant plant manager, you have carefully analyzed the
plant problem, and you have concluded that the fault lies with management's unwillingness to look at the union problems objectively.
You feel that much of the trouble stems from Tom Harper's reluctance
to deal with the union leaders on a fair basis.

You feel that what is needed is a thorough management training
program on how to deal with union problems. You also believe that
if the union were invited to contribute ideas and suggestions, and
to generally participate in improving plant performance, the situation would straighten itself out.

You, yourself, were in a labor union, and you believe that
labor unions are a vital force for good in plant situations. You
feel that Dan Maurice has tried to be a good union president, but
because he has been blocked by management, he has been forced to
become militant. You would like to see Mr. Maurice consulted by
management as a partner in improving plant performance.

Play this role in the Wednesday morning meeting. You are free
to say anything or advocate any solution to plant problems that
will fit within the general context of this role.

ROLE FOR AL WHITWORTH

As press department foreman, you hate the union, union leaders,
and Mr. Maurice in particular. You feel that the work stoppage in
your department has placed you on the spot with Mr. Harper, and
you would like to stand firm against giving anything to the union.

OLYMPIC CORPORATION

Play this role in the Wednesday morning meeting. You are
free to try anything or say anything that will fit within the
general context of this role.

CASE 76

PETRI CHEMICAL COMPANY (D): HOWARD EVANS

This case might have been placed in any number of places in the text. But since it has union-management overtones, it was placed in the Employee Representation section.

Howard Evans's complaint probably would be legitimate, even if he did not have a union representing him in this situation. The basic issue focuses on management's efforts to maintain flexibility of its work force and Evans's unhappiness over the excessive rotation of jobs. Evans feels that he is getting a "raw deal" because he does not have the pick of the jobs he would like to have.

The union contract's Sections 1 and 21 are interesting to compare. Section 1 seems to give management the right to transfer employees in any way management wishes. However, Section 21-b seems to limit that right somewhat by providing employees with an opportunity to express preferences for various job openings and situations.

What should Foreman Roger Lester do? Should he refer the grievance to higher management or to the personnel department? What can be done to placate Howard Evans and again stimulate his previous excellent work performance? Should new bargaining efforts with the union be explored to develop a better way to handle the question of work assignments? These are some of the knotty questions that students should be expected to grapple with here.

CASE 77

THE DISPUTED OVERTIME WORK

This case illustrates the type of problem that can arise when a supervisor tries to be a considerate person, but in the process violates or in some way abridges a policy or practice that normally is followed. Well-established practices are often considered to be almost as binding on management as are the specific provisions of a union contract. In this case the union has been quick to take advantage of an awkward situation to press a grievance alleging that the company violated an agreed-upon past practice.

DISCUSSION QUESTIONS

1. If Mary Caldwell had worked the entire Saturday shift without having talked with her foreman, would she have been entitled to payment for the unscheduled work on her part? Why or why not?
2. Was Alex Burns entitled to overtime pay under the practice of offering overtime to employees in accordance with their seniority and ability? Why or why not?
3. Evaluate the company's argument that the claim of the union was unjust and inequitable. Evaluate the company's further argument that no union employee, including Burns, incurred any loss of work or income because the company acted in a considerate manner.

After thoroughly discussing this case in terms of what management should do in response to the union grievance, the instructor may wish to inform the class/students that (1) the company continued to deny the union grievance and (2) the union then proceeded to appeal the case all the way to arbitration. To the company's dismay, the arbitrator in the case decided in favor of the union position. In reaching his decision, the arbitrator commented as follows:

> The Arbitrator does not feel that by allowing Burns 16 hours' pay he is penalizing the Company. He rather feels that in finding Burns is entitled to the pay, he is doing no more than upholding the agreement the Company made with the Union.

171

Burns should be paid for the shift worked by
the employee with less seniority and at the
prevailing rate for said shift.

CASE 78

THE RELUCTANT JUNK MAN

Interest in writing this case was initiated as a result of a meeting between one of the authors and the director of industrial relations of the Santa Fe Company. This official served as arbitrator in a mock arbitration in a graduate seminar in industrial relations. In the discussion of other cases in which he had been involved, this one was of interest to the author.

PRINCIPAL ISSUES

o Industrial relations
o Personnel administration
o Interdepartmental communication
o Reporting procedures

SYNOPSIS

Plant management has discharged an employee for theft. The employee has grieved his discharge through the negotiated grievance procedure and been turned down at all stages until the last one, arbitration. The arbitrator must decide if the employee was discharged in accordance with terms of the contract.

TEACHING OBJECTIVES

This case examines the problems faced by both management and the union in preparing a case for arbitration. The primary objective of the case is to give the student a better understanding of the arbitration process. The case is suitable for a mock arbitration hearing with students role playing management, the union, and witnesses. An outsider may be brought in as arbitrator, since it is difficult to assume the roles of teacher and arbitrator. The students have trouble thinking of the instructor in any other role than instructor. The case is well suited to labor relations courses. It may also be used in business policy and personnel administration courses.

This teaching note was prepared by Professor William V. Rice, Jr., and Professor Robert McGlashan of the School of Business and Public Administration of the University of Houston at Clear Lake City. Used by permission.

DISCUSSION QUESTIONS

1. What is the issue here?
2. How much weight should you give the confession of Mr. Brown?
3. Should Mr. Grey's record of twenty-five years service with the company be a consideration?
4. Should management have given more direct supervision to Mr. Grey?
5. You are the arbitrator. Give your decision and justify your award.

COMMENTS ON THE DISCUSSION QUESTIONS

1. The central question is whether Mr. Grey was, as alleged by the company, a party to the theft and sale of several loads of scrap material belonging to the company at various times during his tenure as salvage yard operator, and one load in particular on August 11, 1976. If so, does such conduct constitute proper cause for discharge?

    The students could (may) want to try Mr. Brown and Mr. Grey on criminal charges of felony theft. That is not the purpose of this hearing. It is simply to determine if there is just cause for the discharge and if the discharge was in accordance with the terms of the contract.

2. The instructor might want to make some additional facts available to the students (perhaps only if the students are perceptive enough to ask) regarding Mr. Brown and his testimony.

    a. Mr. Brown had also been selling scrap belonging to Ultramarine and implicated other employees of Ultramarine. Over a period of some six months Mr. Brown admitted receiving 21 checks, 11 from Golden Rule and 10 from another scrap dealer. These checks were all payable to "J. Brown," dated at various times beginning in March 1976 and ending with the Golden Rule check that was in payment for the load of August 11. Mr. Brown verified receipt of these checks and admitted hauling the scrap material from the Santa Fe plant, some directly from the Ultramarine project and some from the Santa Fe salvage yard operated by Mr. Grey.

    b. The only Santa Fe material absolutely identified was from the load of August 11. Even though Mr. Brown testified to other loads, none of the material was available in the Golden Rule Yard, so the case hinges on the August 11 load.

    c. In oral testimony during the hearings, Mr. Brown was not a "good" witness. He changed his story several times after his arrest, and his testimony at the hearing was inconsistent. Moreover, the company had entered into an agreement with him to drop criminal charges in exchange for his testimony against Mr. Grey. Therefore, he had much to gain and little to lose by testifying against Mr. Grey.

    d.   The arbitrator agreed with the union's position that clear
and uncontrovertible evidence is necessary to support a
discharge. The discharged employee must be guilty of the
alleged offense beyond a reasonable doubt.

    e. Mr. Brown's testimony does not satisfy the usual tests of
credibility and, standing alone, would not be sufficient to
substantiate the discharge of Mr. Grey.

3. Perhaps the appropriate place for a consideration of Mr. Grey's
service record would have been by the company in determining
whether or not to discharge Mr. Grey. Now that this decision
has been made, the role of the arbitrator is to ascertain if
there was a just cause for discharge and if it was done in
accordance with the contract. Arbitrators are usually very
reluctant to substitute their definitions of "mercy" for that
of the company, but confine their decisions to the question
of whether or not proper cause for discipline exists.

4. The obvious answer, looking back, is that management should
have given more supervision to Mr. Grey. Material could have
been saved and perhaps more importantly, an employee of twenty-
five years service could have been saved from temptation.
But because Mr. Grey had been an outstanding employee, management felt that he would do a good job as salvage yard operator.
Needless to say, management has tightened supervision of the
salvage yard and also security provided by the plant gate
guards.

5. As indicated earlier, the testimony of Mr. Brown standing alone
would not be enough to justify an award against Mr. Grey. But
two pieces of circumstantial evidence tend to support Mr.
Brown's testimony.

      The first involves the process of loading and removing
scrap from the salvage yard and the time required. While Mr.
Brown's allegations that several prior loads were taken from
the Santa Fe salvage yard are unsupported by other evidence,
it was established that the load of August 11 was Santa Fe
property and that very likely it came from the salvage yard.

      A fork-lift truck, winch truck, or similar piece of heavy
equipment would have been required to load the material, which
consisted of a large gear and other pieces of machinery, each
weighing 400 lbs. or more. The time required to load this
equipment was estimated to be between 30 minutes and an hour
and a half. Thus, either Mr. Grey loaded the material or
absented himself for this time interval at the precise time
the truck was loaded, conveniently leaving the fork lift for
the thieves during this period. If not, it would have been
necessary for Mr. Brown to have brought along a fork lift or
similar equipment (in addition to the flatbed truck) at precisely the time of Mr. Grey's absence from the yard, and, too,
would have required some assurance that Mr. Grey's absence
would be of the required duration. This latter operation would

probably have required an accomplice. The union offered no evidence that Mr. Grey was absent from the salvage yard for <u>any</u> appreciable period of time on August 11. The second circumstance tending to implicate Mr. Grey is Detective White's testimony that Mr. Grey stated in his oral confession that he had received $160 from Mr. Brown as his share of the August 11 sale and that this was his (Detective White's) first knowledge of the $160 transaction. Detective White testified that it was not until Mr. Grey had been sent to the polygraph room that Mr. Brown was brought from jail for interrogation and alleged that he had given Mr. Grey $160 as his share. Mr. Grey denies this and stated that the police officer must have told him that Mr. Brown so testified. Again we have Mr. Grey's word against that of another witness, but Detective White is the more credible of the two. He was a straightforward witness with nothing to gain or lose by testifying.

Mr. Grey's oral confession to the police officer is neither logical nor rational for an innocent man. The logical and probable reaction of an innocent man who finds himself falsely accused is anger and righteous indignation. Mr. Grey and the union argue that the confession was a clever ruse to avoid spending the weekend in jail. Here again it is unreasonable to believe that a rational man would risk disgrace and a long prison term to avoid a weekend in custody. Of even more significance is the fact that Mr. Grey had available a much more reliable, logical, and straightforward way to secure his release, if he were <u>innocent</u>, and one recommended to him by both his attorney and policy officers: taking the polygraph test.

The arbitrator is therefore forced to the conclusion that Mr. Buford Grey was guilty and when confronted with the polygraph test elected to confess rather than go through with the test, which he feared would reveal his guilt. While not necessary to this conclusion, the circumstantial evidence does support it.

AWARD

The discharge of Mr. Buford Grey was for proper cause and is sustained.

NOTE TO INSTRUCTORS

The award and much of the rationale are taken from the actual case. From several years of holding mock arbitration hearings and working arbitration cases, it has been the experience of the authors that the students want to know the award in the actual case. The instructor should be cautioned that if the case is used as a mock arbitration, the arbitrator could very well hold for Mr. Grey. It has been our experience that in a mock arbitration hearing the arbitrator <u>may</u> rule in opposition to the actual ruling. This is usually because the "losing" (losing side in the actual case) side worked harder and presented their witnesses more skillfully than the "winning" side. If this occurs we suggest that you point out what could have been done and where other evidence could have been presented and witnesses called. We suggest that you do not stress "winning" or "losing," although this is generally important to the students in a mock hearing, but instead emphasize that most of the learning takes place in the preparation and presentation of the case regardless of who wins or loses.

CASE 79

DID THE EMPLOYEE "REFUSE TO WORK"?

This case was an actual arbitration case heard by one of the
authors of this text. The case is presented in a convenient format
to depict the principal issues and the arguments of the company
and the union.

One way to use this case is to divide the class into small
groups and have them discuss the case independently. Then ask them
to reach a decision in the case, as a labor arbitrator would be
required to do.

Another way of approaching this case is to utilize the arbitration simulation approach described earlier in this manual on pages
8-9.

Students usually like to compare their decisions with that of
the arbitrator. The decision of the arbitrator is included here in
part for the purposes of comparison only. However, the instructor
should be careful to point out that whatever decisions the students
reach independently should not be considered either right or wrong
in comparison with that of the arbitrator.

EXCERPTS FROM THE ARBITRATOR'S DECISION (ALL NAMES DISGUISED)

An employee is obligated to carry out a work assignment that
is legitimate and permissible under the Agreement. If the employee
feels that it is an unfair assignment, the employee has the duty
to do the assignment, and then may file a grievance under the
grievance procedure. In the case before the Arbitrator, there
is no question that Company management had the right to ask Ms.
Donovan to do the work of the filler job classification. Even
though the filler work was a higher classified job, the Company
had the right under Article XXII of the Agreement to require Ms.
Donovan to do the work at her normal rate of pay on a temporary
basis (i.e., up to ten days). Ms. Donovan claimed that she did
not know how to do the work. The company presented evidence and
testimony to the effect that Ms. Donovan did know how to do the
work, and that she had done similar work previously. However,
employee statements presented by the Union representative cast
doubt as to whether or not Ms. Donovan knew how to do the filler
work; or if she did, that she could only do the filler work in a
limited fashion.

178

Although the evidence is far from clear and not totally convincing, the Arbitrator is inclined to believe that Ms. Donovan was obligated to and could have proceeded to begin work on the filler job. If she experienced problems, she could have asked for help from the foreman or lead man. In the Arbitrator's view, it was Ms. Donovan's duty to attempt the work and to call for help if it was necessary. Rather, she took a stubborn point of view, claiming that she did not know how to do the work, and she continued to work at her regular job assignment. To the Arbitrator, Ms. Donovan was definitely guilty of an act of insubordination, and therefore the Company was well within its rights to initiate disciplinary action against her.

Having concluded that Ms. Donovan was guilty of an act of insubordination, the Arbitrator next must evaluate if the Company's discharge action was appropriate considering the whole pattern of circumstances in the Sangamon Cabinet Company plant.

It is the Arbitrator's view--given all the circumstances in the case--that the penalty of discharge was extremely severe. The Arbitrator believes that the Company did not present clear and convincing proof that under all the circumstances of the situation the ultimate penalty of discharge was both reasonable and appropriate. A number of mitigating circumstances in the case lead the Arbitrator to conclude that a lesser penalty should be substantiated for the penalty of discharge. These mitigating circumstances were: (1) the failure of the Union shop steward to properly counsel Ms. Donovan; (2) the question as to whether or not Ms. Donovan could really do the work in question; and (3) the fact that there was no evidence of any progressive disciplinary approach taken at the Company concerning Ms. Donovan--or any other employees at the plant for that matter. Nevertheless, Ms. Donovan was guilty of a serious infraction of the labor Agreement and of generally accepted standards of employee performance. In the Arbitrator's view, her behavior requires a major disciplinary penalty, which should serve as a clear signal to Ms. Donovan and other employees concerning the importance of carrying out their legitimate work responsibilities.

Arbitrator's Award

1. Based upon all of the foregoing, the Arbitrator finds that the discharge penalty meted out against Ms. Marie Donovan was excessive, and the discharge is rescinded.

2. The Arbitrator finds that a disciplinary suspension of extended duration is an appropriate remedy in this case situation. The Arbitrator believes that a disciplinary suspension without pay of approximately six weeks duration should serve to impress on Ms. Donovan and other employees in the plant the serious nature of the consequences for failure to carry out a legitimate work assignment. Therefore, the Arbitrator directs that Ms. Donovan shall remain on disciplinary suspension without pay until February 17, 19--. At that time, he directs that Ms. Donovan shall be returned to her position as Class "D" employee, or some equivalent position in the Company as job availabilities

permit. The Arbitrator further directs that Ms. Donovan's seniority rights shall be restored in full.

3. It should be understood by the Company, the Union, and Ms. Donovan that any subsequent acts of insubordination or serious unsatisfactory conduct on the part of Ms. Donovan may lead to immediate and permanent discharge.

CASE 80

THE RECALL FROM LAYOFF CONTROVERSY

This arbitration case, like the preceding case, "Did the Employee 'Refuse to Work'?" was heard by one of the authors of this text. See the discussion concerning Case 79 for suggestions on how to use an arbitration-type case in a classroom setting.

EXCERPTS FROM THE ARBITRATOR'S DECISION (ALL NAMES DISGUISED)

In analyzing the various sections of the Agreement cited by both the Union and the Company, the Arbitrator believes that none of these sections is directly applicable to the issue involved in arbitration. Article VIII, Section 4 covers primarily the employer's requirement to notify employees by posting when they are to be laid off, but it does not specifically address itself to the question of how a recall notice shall be carried out. There is an implied analogy that posting shall be the proper way to carry out recall notification, but this is not explicit.

In the Arbitrator's opinion, Article VIII, Section 7 does not apply to the case, since it only involves notification of an employee who is being terminated permanently. Similarly, Article XXVII, Section 2 seems to apply to the situation of an employee who has been absent for some reason other than layoff, such as sickness. Further, this section is somewhat ambiguous, since it speaks of the requirement of the employee to notify a supervisor of his intention to return to work; yet later in the same section there is an implication that he may have been notified by the Company to report to work from an absence!

Thus the Arbitrator believes that there are no provisions in the Agreement which he can utilize for clear guidance in his decision, and therefore he must next look to the question of past practices between the Company and Union. Here, too, the evidence is conflicting. Company testimony that most employees prefer to call in much of the time is quite compelling evidence to the Arbitrator. On the other hand, the Company admits that on numerous occasions it does take the initiative to attempt to call employees to notify them to report to work from layoff. Certainly, this mixed procedure could be rather confusing to employees in the absence of any clear statement concerning their responsibility one way or the other.

Further, during testimony in the hearing there was no evidence presented that would clearly indicate to the Arbitrator that all employees, particularly employee George Vervack in this case, were aware of a definite obligation on their part to call in to the Company or dispatcher to inquire about work assignments from layoff. Apparently, Mr. Vervack did not believe he was obligated to do so, although presumably he now does call in as a result of this particular experience.

It appears to the Arbitrator that the Company did feel some obligation to notify Mr. Vervack by its action on the Monday morning in question. If the Company felt that it did not have such an obligation, why did it bother to call Mr. Vervack at 8 a.m. that Monday morning? Presumably, if the Company felt that since Mr. Vervack had not shown up, and that he had made no effort to find out whether he should show up, the Company could immediately have selected the next man on layoff from the seniority list. However, the Company apparently felt it did have some obligation to try at that point to call Mr. Vervack to tell him that he should report to work. This, in the Arbitrator's opinion, demonstrates that the practice of posting versus telephoning versus calling in was confusing even in the minds of Company officials.

In other words, the Arbitrator does not have clear evidence of a past practice that was mutually agreed upon and understood by both of the parties involved. The preponderance of evidence suggests to the Arbitrator that most employees took it upon themselves to call in to the Company to check regarding work assignments from layoff, but apparently not all of the employees did so and the Company also frequently attempted to notify employees by telephone rather than simply using the posting mechanism. Who, then, definitely is obligated to take the initiative to make sure that the proper communication has taken place in this situation?

The Arbitrator, being unable to be clearly guided by the Agreement or past practices, must next look to a third test which arbitrators normally utilize in adjudicating situations such as the type involved in the present grievance. This test is simply one of equity and fairness, although such a test usually resolves itself in the "eye of the beholder." In deciding issues predominantly from the standpoint of equity and fairness when no other guidance is clearly available, this Arbitrator has tended to place the burden of demonstration of fairness on the Company, rather than on the employee. If the Company in this case had attempted to call Mr. Vervack at any time on the Friday preceding the Monday recall assignment—even if they had been unable to contact Mr. Vervack by telephone that day—the Arbitrator certainly believes that it would have fulfilled whatever obligation it might have had to notify Mr. Vervack. Why the Company in this instance did not attempt to call Mr. Vervack on Friday was not clear. Mr. Thompson stated that it was an oversight, or perhaps it was simply a matter of being preoccupied with other activities.

In this instance, the Arbitrator is inclined to believe that the Company did not go the "extra mile" which it could have done in order to totally fulfill whatever obligation it might have had

to notify Mr. Vervack of his work assignment. The existing practices in the Company were unclear and somewhat confusing, and they
probably reflected the difficult economic situation of the Company
at this point in time. Nevertheless, the Arbitrator feels that
equity in this situation compels him to sustain the grievance of
Mr. Vervack, although he is still not certain as to whether or not
Mr. Vervack was aware of any obligation on his part to call in to
the Company to inquire about a work assignment.

Arbitrator's Decision

Based upon all the foregoing, the Arbitrator rules as follows:

1. That part of the Union grievance relating to George Vervack is
   sustained. The Arbitrator directs that George Vervack shall
   be made whole for one day's pay which he would have received if
   he would have been notified by the Company and had worked on
   the Monday in question.

2. That part of the Union grievance requesting that the Company
   "cease its present practice" concerning notifying employees
   of recall from layoff is denied. The Arbitrator would emphasize that his decision in this matter is limited solely to the
   case of Mr. Vervack, and it should not in any way be construed
   as a requirement on the Company that it must attempt to telephone or otherwise change its existing practices of posting
   and/or calling employees directly to inform them of recall
   from layoff.

3. In connection with #2 above, the Arbitrator feels that although
   the current practices in ths Company are somewhat confusing,
   any determination of a firm policy agreement in this regard must be left to the parties themselves. The Arbitrator
   strongly recommends, although he cannot direct such action,
   that representatives of the Company and the Union meet to determine and agree on a specific procedure to cover the question
   of notification of employees from layoff. In the Arbitrator's
   view, any such specific agreement should consider both the
   desires of the employees and the realistic problems attendant
   to the Company operation.

PART EIGHT

PERSONNEL/HUMAN RESOURCES MANAGEMENT POLICY STATEMENTS

GENERAL COMMENTARY

In the introductory text to Part Eight, the authors presented their thoughts and observations concerning the purpose and meaning of personnel/human resources management policy statements.

Instructors may choose to use these policy statements for varied objectives. The policy statements might be assigned merely for reading to illustrate how companies and other organizations verbalize their policies concerning personnel/human resources management. Or they can be used as types of "cases." Instructors will find that policy statements can stimulate much group discussion, particularly if the instructor has students focus their thinking on such considerations as the following:

1. How each policy statement reflects the nature (product, objectives, competitive position, etc.) of the company or group stating the policy
2. Differing points of emphasis in these statements and the varying degrees of acceptance of these policies by managers, supervisors, and employees
3. How these statements reflect cultural beliefs, mores, and norms
4. Whether these statements are mere "window dressing" or reflect the reality of actual day-to-day personnel relationships

PART NINE

ADDITIONAL CASES

NOTE TO INSTRUCTORS

For the convenience of instructors who may wish to use a case or cases for examination or other classroom-related purposes, we are providing several additional cases in this Instructor's Manual. Adopters of Cases and Policies in Personnel/Human Resources Management--Fifth Edition are authorized to reproduce the following cases for examination and classroom purposes:

81. Vanzo Manufacturing Company
82. The Bypassed Supervisor
83. The College Protestor
84. Tardy Too Often

Teaching notes or commentaries are also provided for each of these cases.

CASE 81

VANZO MANUFACTURING COMPANY

You have recently received your baccalaureate degree from a prestigious public college in upstate New York. Because of your extensive background in personnel management, you landed a position as assistant to the president of the Vanzo Manufacturing Company (VMC), a medium-sized manufacturing firm located in Westchester County. You are presently seated in the office of the president during your first day on the job, and she is providing you with a historical rundown of VMC prior to your scheduled meeting with the primary personnel and other staff members.

Ms. Vanzo, the founder and principal stock owner of the company, leans back in her comfortable executive chair and says to you, "You know, this is my company, and I'm responsible for where we are today. There aren't many managers who can say that today in these times of giant conglomerates. I have hand-picked my staff, who you'll meet very soon, and we've kind of grown up together. You are the first new executive-level employee we've hired in 12 years. I suspect you may encounter some unintended resistance because of our family style of management. Our fiscal year 82-83 sales projections mandate that we closely scrutinize our total business organization. Of particular interest and importance to me are our current personnel policies and procedures. For your first assignment, I want you to examine where we are now and then determine action plans to get us where we need to be. Our personnel practices will be a key factor in our reaching the fiscal year 82-83 strategic goals. I must alert you to the fact that our personnel department is currently at odds with several other departments. Keep an open mind and let me know what you think. I'm really looking forward to big things from you, and I seriously hope your analysis can assist us. It is obvious that we need to do a great deal of management hiring at this location and blue-collar hiring at our newly purchased southern plant. We need that plant for its inexpensive labor, and it eliminates some union problems up here. I also have a keen interest in really assessing my performance appraisal system. Since we all have worked together

This case was prepared by Jeffrey A. McNally (Major, U.S. Army), Department of Behavioral Sciences and Leadership, U.S. Military Academy, as a basis for class discussion rather than to illustrate effective or ineffective handling of an administrative situation. Used by permission.

for so long, I do not conduct performance appraisals for my top
V.P.s. I'm afraid, though, that some of them are slipping. I feel
that we need to shake things up to meet our financial goals for
fiscal year 82-83. I'm having my weekly meeting with my V.P.s in
a few minutes; let's get some coffee and go down to the conference
room."

Before you head to the conference room, Ms. Vanzo provides
you with the following information about VMC.

Work force   553 employees, 96 management/white-collar employees and 457 blue-collar employees. An additional 300 blue-
collar employees are currently on layoff and will probably not be
recalled. Of the 96 management employees, 95 percent are male and
5 percent are female. Of the 457 blue-collar employees, the male/
female distribution is 54 percent/46 percent. About 8 percent are
minorities. A UAW union, Local 36002, is the bargaining unit
for all blue-collar employees at the Westchester facility. Approximately 82 percent of the blue-collar employees are union
members.

In 1979 Vanzo purchased a 250,000-square-foot facility in the
South. This plant has the capability and capacity to make the same
products as the Westchester plant and to do it more efficiently.
This plant currently employs 250 blue-collar workers. There is no
labor union at this plant.

Sales

FY 79-80	$49.2 million
FY 80-81	51.7 million
FY 81-82	53.1 million
FY 82-83	90.0 million (projected- current business plan)

Profits

FY 79-80	$5.1 million
FY 80-81	5.3 million
FY 81-82	5.5 million
FY 82-83	9.0 million (projected- current business plan)

Technology   Assembly-line production with specialization.
Currently undergoing large-plant, automation studies.

Strategic goals   To produce, market, and distribute high-
quality replacement automobile parts, such as manifold gaskets,
rotars, etc., for sale to small automobile distributors and service

stations. (Products generally sell for $10-20 per item.) To
increase sales by 70 percent in FY 82-83 and 30 percent in FY 83-84;
to increase profits by 60 percent in FY 82-83 and 35 percent in
FY 83-84.

Market   Small automobile distributors and service stations in
the New England area. Special targets are new distributors and
service stations. Company has been quite successful in picking up
several large volume distributors in the past eight months.

A few minutes later in the day, you and Ms. Vanzo arrive in
the VMC conference room, and she makes the following introductory
remarks:

"For the benefit of my new assistant, who is here with us
for the first day, I have asked each of our personnel staff
members to present an informal, candid overview of their area
of responsibility. Let me start the ball rolling by saying
that from the executive suite this company seems to have come
a long way. But as you all know, I'm not the sort of individual who likes to sit still for very long. We've had good,
strong real economic growth over the last several years, but
I feel now the time is right for us to make a really significant
effort toward growth and expansion. Now is the time for hard
work.

"Somehow we need to energize the Vanzo Manufacturing Company,
because our growth objectives are ambitious, but attainable. I
know all of us are anxious about our upcoming negotiations with
Local 36002. I want you all to know that I will make it as
difficult as I can for the union. Samuel Johnson, our second
shift foreman and the chief union steward, has been transferred
to the graveyard shift. This should hamper their negotiation
preparations. Also, as most of you know, many of our recent 300
layoffs are strong, and vocal, pro-union members. That is of
course no coincidence. We'll have to learn to live with union
interference, but I'm certainly not going to treat the union as
an equal. They can ask for all they want, but VMC is not their
company. Unfortunately, the union will no doubt increase our
standard operating costs, though.

"Speaking of operating costs, I have recently noticed that
our absentee, tardiness, and quality control wastage rates have
been way too high. I recall that when I was heading production
during our first years of business, we experienced similar problems,
which we overcame with stringent crackdown on offenders. I think
we ought to consider adopting some of the same measures now. I
think we ought to begin to promote those employees who are never
absent or tardy and consistently better the quality control wastage
rates, and we will get rid of those employees who cannot measure
up. There's certainly no need to do any of this management by
objectives stuff; that's a bureaucratic nightmare if I've ever
seen one. Let's not publicize this policy change, but I can
assure you the word will get around quickly enough. I'm not one

to get all hung up with job descriptions and specifications. We know who's doing, and not doing, their jobs. After all, this is my company.

"Another thing that has been bothering me is our community relations. Various groups in Westchester County and some government agencies like the EEOC have been trying to put pressure on Vanzo Manufacturing to hire additional minorities. Well . . . poppycock! No one tells VMC what to do. We are, and always have been, in the business of making money by making our customers happy. Our responsibility is to our customers and ourselves-- nobody else. What, for example, do our customers care about the sexual and racial distribution of our work force? All these EEO laws really do not apply to us, because we are covered with our current mix of employees. Well . . . I've gone on much longer than I had expected. But, as you all know, I do tend to ramble.

"For the benefit of my new assistant, let me introduce each of you, and then we can roll up our sleeves and get to work. First our vice president of personnel, Mr. Milton Chance. Next, Milt's right hand man, Mr. William Donalds, and the third member of our personnel staff, Mr. Harold Thomas. Also, Ray Anderson, our V.P. for manufacturing; Roger Hartell, our V.P. for marketing; and Mike Klubier, our V.P. for quality assurance. Milt, I realize you have responsibility for much of what we are interested in today, so why don't you begin."

"Boss," Milton Chance begins, "I must agree with you that the union has made life increasingly difficult for us all. Although our contract negotiations are three months away, I'm already having to do a lot of analysis of the issues.

"Let me give everyone a brief overview of our union situation. The employees of the company were not formed into a union until 1964. In that year, as a result of the campaign to organize the mass production industries, the union established itself. It was victorious in an NLRB election, and the certification as a result of the election was awarded to Local 36002 on January 20, 1965. From that date, Local 36002 has represented the production and maintenance workers of the company.

"Only one strike has taken place since the union came into the picture; it occurred in 1970. The issues of the strike were the union's demand for a union shop, increased wages, and additional paid holidays. The strike lasted six weeks, and when it terminated the union obtained for its members a six-cents hourly wage increase and three more paid holidays, although they had initially demanded eleven cents per hour and eight more paid holidays. The union failed in its attempt to obtain any arrangement requiring membership in the union as a condition of employment. Also, the current contract does not include a checkoff.

"The average wage in the plant is $8.96 per hour, which is of course well in excess of minimum wage. The plant involved in the negotiations is our Westchester County location. Our new plant in Little Rock, Arkansas, produces the same items. It was purchased in 1979 and now employs 250 workers. Efforts to organize the southern plants have not been successful. The average rate in the nonunion plant is $5.40 per hour. During the last eight months 300 employees in the Westchester plant have been laid off. It is no secret that the reason for this has been the increase of output in the Arkansas plant.

"The company works on a three-shift basis, paying $20 and $25 premiums for the second and third shifts, although it customarily operates on two shifts and only on occasion operates the third shift. Employees work a standard 40-hour work week. If employees work in excess of 40 hours per week, we have not up to this point paid any sort of overtime wages. It really has not seemed necessary, and no one has complained. On the first two shifts the company operates all its departments, which means an equal division of the labor force on the two shifts. When it operates a third shift, it operates only the departments needed to fill pressing orders. In the last three years it operated a third shift only on 70 working days.

"In general, the relations between the management and the union have been satisfactory, although there have, of course, been the usual disagreements. However, in the last year there have been two "wildcat" strikes, participated in by some of the workers in the oil pump department. In both cases the union disclaimed all responsibility for the strikes and alleged that it did what it could to get the workers back to their jobs. The first wildcat strike lasted two days and the second, four days. There is an absolute no-strike clause in the present contract, and the company threatened to sue the union for damages under the terms of the Taft-Hartley Act, the company claiming that the first violation of the contract cost it $75,000 in damages and the second, $185,000. However, the company finally decided not to sue. No one was disciplined because of the strike. There was also a very brief incident in 1976 when a new, generally unknown union attempted to gain recognition and replace Local 36002. It was a very confusing time with a lot of allegations and counter-allegations. There was also during this period a brief jurisdictional strike that lasted several days.

"The existing contract contains a standard grievance procedure and provides for arbitration of all disputes arising under the contract, except for those pertaining to production standards. Management has the unilateral right to establish production standards according to the grievances that were filed by employees generally protesting against "unreasonably" high production standards. As required by the contract, the company negotiated the production standard grievances, but the union did not have the right to appeal to arbitration or to strike over them. The management's rights clause states, in effect, that the company retains all rights except as limited by other provisions of the labor agreement.

"The seniority clause provides for promotions to be based on length of service and ability. During the contract period 21 grievances were filed by employees who protested against the company's filling jobs with junior service employees. The company's position in these grievances was that the junior employees had more ability than the senior employees. Five of these grievances went to arbitration, the company winning four of them and the union winning one. Promotions are bid for on a departmental basis.

"The seniority area of the existing contract also provides for plant-wide application of seniority credits for layoffs and recalls. During the recent period in which many layoffs occurred because of declining sales, the company, as required by the contract, laid off many junior employees rather than the senior employees who had to be retained. Many foremen requested management to take action in the next negotiations to remedy this situation.

"Last year, union stewards spent on the average about ten hours per week on grievance work for which they were paid by the company. There are no limitations on stewards performing such grievance work. Foremen have complained that some stewards are goofing off, using "union business" as a pretext not to work. Typically all stewards deny what the foremen say. In fact, the stewards claim that it is the unreasonable attitude of foremen that provokes grievances and complaints. Also, the stewards claim that there cannot be a true measure of their time on the basis of the number of written grievances filed, since a good share of their time is spent discussing grievances orally with employees and and with first- and second-line supervisors before a written grievance is filed. There is no record showing how many of these oral discussions alleviated problems without written grievances being filed.

"Last year, because of an unexpected order from the government, the plant worked overtime for a period of two weeks. Under the existing contract, the company has the right to require overtime. About 200 employees refused to work overtime and only did work because the company threatened to fire them if they refused. It has been rumored that these 200 employees have been causing a lot of trouble in the union about this overtime affair. In addition, according to the contract, the company has the right to select the employees who are to work overtime, and some employees have claimed that the foremen are not being fair and are giving their personal friends the opportunity to earn the extra money and discriminating against the other employees.

"For many years each skilled tradesman has worked only within his or her trade. There are five trades hired: mechanics, carpenters, tool and die workers, plumbers, and electricians. Five months ago the company required a mechanic to do a job normally performed by a plumber. The employee and union filed a grievance and the case went all the way to arbitration. The arbitrator sustained the position of the union on the basis of the "past practice" principle. Altogether the company hired about 175 skilled tradesmen. Their average rate is $10.31 per hour. Skilled tradesmen have been affected by the current layoff. Twenty-five of them are laid off. They charge that the company has been subcontracting out skilled worked that could be done in the shop. Under the current contract there is no restriction on the company's right to subcontract.

"The present contract was negotiated for a three-year period. Both sides indicated during the contractual period that they may want to move away from this long-term arrangement in the future for a variety of reasons. However, there is no assurance that this attitude indicated a sincere position on the part of the parties or that it was merely an expression of a possible bargaining position.

"Automation has been a problem in the company for a period of several years. About 250 workers have been permanently separated because of automation. Union and management meetings to deal with the problem during the past several years have proven fruitless. Previous discussions have centered around the rate of automation, the problem of the displaced employees, training of employees for the jobs created by automation, and seniority systems. All indications are that the next wave of automation will cost about 90 blue-collar jobs. Part of the rumor is that the company intends to hire employees from the outside to run these new machines. The 250 employees who have been permanently separated are in addition to the current 300 employees who are on layoff because of the southern situation.

"There also is a problem involving "working rules." These include: a 15-minute rest period every four hours, no change in the number of employees to jobs unless the job technology is substantially changed, paid lunch periods for scheduled or un-scheduled overtime that exceeds four hours, and paid "wash-up" time for 10 minutes prior to quitting time. The company contends that these working rules are costing considerable money. Whenever this issue has been brought up in the past, the union has resisted any change.

"During the last several weeks most employees have been wearing buttons and armbands stating: "We want total job security." A few days ago the company posted many large signs stating: "The best way to achieve job security is through more production. Go! Go! Go!" Now, the union wants these signs taken down on the grounds that they are causing fear and confusion among its members. In addition, the union found out that the posters were printed in a nonunion shop.

"We tentatively plan to greatly increase our southern plant work force to meet our budgeted fiscal year 82-83 growth. However, we have encountered some unexpected problems. Local 36002 is currently conducting an authorization-card-signing drive in our southern plant, seeking to obtain the required 30 percent of signed authorization cards. We are going to oppose this with all the means at our disposal. For a start we will bar card-signing drives from the plant just like we keep everyone else out. Local 36002 can set up a booth in the parking lot just like the United Way did last month. We plan to raise wages by about $.50 an hour during the card-signing drive. This should make people think twice about just what advantages they get for their union dues.

If Local 36002 gets their 30 percent, I have had our lawyers prepare a very strong argument that the shipping department should
not be part of the bargaining unit. There are a lot of union
supporters in that area and I would like to split them off from
the others. During the election we will hire an advertising firm
that will structure a campaign around the question: "What can the
union do for you that Vanzo Corporation cannot do?" Of course,
this has an impact on upcoming contract negotiations at our
northern plant.

"I expect the negotiations at the northern plant to focus
primarily on wages, security clauses, and fringe benefits, because
they said something to this effect in a letter I received last
week. The union notified us of these issues in writing, although
I do not think they needed to be this formal. They want to have
some preliminary meetings before the actual negotiations begin,
but like you, Boss, I want to make things as difficult for them
as possible. We know what they want now, but I'm not going to
give them a clue to our positions, and I'm certainly not going to
meet with any of them until I absolutely must. I intend to go
into those negotiations and fight for every point. I know that we
will have to concede some things; however, I intend to get something for everything I give up. After all, this is a win-lose
relationship. Also, don't forget Sam Johnson talks a very hard
line, but once we get into negotiations he's a pushover. This time
I'm going to back him to the wall and get everything we want. After
all, we have nothing to lose.

"Another major area of concern pressuring our personnel shop
is the ever increasing government interference with VMC's internal
affairs. It's getting ridiculous; let me give you a couple of
examples. I don't mean to correct you Boss, but the EEOC has
been getting involved with our business, and I'm afraid that's
just the law. I'm spending more and more of my time answering correspondence and providing EEO data to federal agencies and com-
missions. We also continue to be bombarded from OSHA. Just keeping
track of their safety guidelines could be a full-time job, and
the guidelines keep changing all the time. In my office I have a
picture of a cowboy after he complied with all of OSHA's safety
standards. That pretty much sums up how I feel about OSHA. I wish
they'd just leave us alone. Sure, we have accidents, but this is
a manufacturing company, and I don't think it's any more dangerous
than a lot of other places. But like EEO, OSHA's also the law, and
I know I must keep all those safety guidelines up-to-date, but
that's all I'm going to do. A lot of companies really go overboard
with safety pamphlets, briefings, motivation campaigns, and the
like, but not us. We simply don't have the staff for it. When
a new employee joins Vanzo Manufacturing, we show him or her how
to operate the machinery carefully. After all, it's in their best
interests not to be injured. The new employees we hire should
help us. Before we purchase any equipment at VMC, we insure that
it is engineered to be as safe as humanly possible. This is very
important to us. I certainly don't think we should waste our money
on safety campaigns and the like.

"With regard to my support for the rest of the firm, I also have noticed the high turnover and absentee rate that production has been experiencing lately, and I have managed to get replacements for all those who have departed. The curious thing is that we're losing so many employees, sometimes within the first couple of weeks. And most of the employees who are leaving are males. Of course, it also seems that most of the turnovers are a bunch of malcontents who only want to get something for nothing. And that won't cut it around here. We pay good wages, not the best, but we pay what we can afford. We meet all the federal and state minimum-wage laws, but we've always got employees complaining. Sure, other companies in the area pay a little more, but they cannot match the prestige of the automobile industry. Money isn't everything. A couple of years ago we had some problems making payroll a couple of times, but that hasn't happened recently. I think some of our folks are a little jittery about the problems with automobile sales, but those folks never should have joined Vanzo Manufacturing. In the short term we may have some problems—— that's the nature of the industry——but in the long haul this is a good, sound company. Once we get our new plant up to speed, maybe the workers here will feel the pressure and try to work harder. We should let people here know how much cheaper it is to produce in the South. This will keep them on their toes.

"Due to our projected growth, I've prepared a tentative organizational chart showing our current management organization and proposed new management hires. I did not really talk with anyone about these employment planning figures, but they seemed to make sense to me." (This chart is shown as Exhibit 81-1.)

Exhibit 81-1

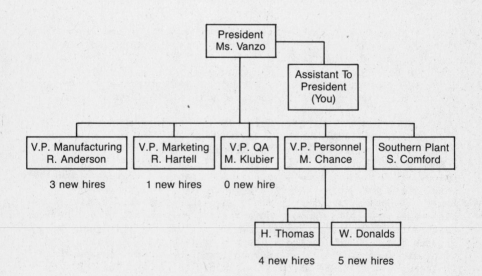

"I realize that this is the first time all of you except Ms. Vanzo have seen this proposal, but I'm sure we can agree on this employment plan. When we get to your part of the meeting, you can comment on Ms. Vanzo's and my proposed fiscal year 82-83 hiring schedule.

"Boss, I may be catching your rambling disease, but I want your new assistant to be aware of the problem I discussed with you yesterday. We may be losing that large Army contract we picked up last year. We don't have the trained personnel to meet the contract specifications. We have to furnish records to the government to show that we have an adequate number of employees with the right technical qualifications who meet the government's Equal Employment Opportunity goals. I simply don't have those kinds of records available at a moment's notice. You know we discussed setting up some sort of a system to look at the supply and demand of our labor force, but we never got around to it. That does it for me, so let me introduce my assistant, Mr. Bill Donalds."

"Milt, before I begin my report let me bring Ms. Vanzo up-to-date on our new, integrated recruiting program we devised. In the past we've just focused our recruiting efforts on the college campuses. Although this has been great for attracting white-collar employees, it really has done nothing for attracting new employees to our blue-collar work force. After all, over 80 percent of our employees are blue-collar workers. This year we plan to continue to recruit at the college campuses, but we will also be contacting the local trade and vocational schools as well as running newspaper and radio advertisements in the Westchester County area as well as around our new plant in the South, where our greatest need for new blue-collar employees exists. We will be attempting to target our recruiting efforts to the particular market we are seeking. We are also considering a cooperative job fair with some of the high schools around the southern plant. This new recruiting strategy should provide a much more integrated way to attract potential employees who can contribute to and also benefit from employment at VMC. I'm really excited about our prospects in this area.

"In addition to recruiting, my main job at VMC is reading regulations and doing most of the writing this office does. I also am responsible for employee training and management development. My major project right now is the complete preparation of job analyses for all the white-collar positions at Vanzo Manufacturing. There doesn't seem to be any purpose to do this for the blue-collar employees. The union will just try to use it against us by saying this or that is not part of their job description. I have been conducting interviews, sending out questionnaires, and of course observing people while they do their jobs. It's a much bigger undertaking than I had anticipated, and its also frustrating. I am doing this only because I have to do it. It's another case of the EEOC and their bona fide occupational requirements. These job analyses are my best efforts to keep those people off our backs. Look, most of our blue-collar employees

have been doing their jobs for years. They certainly do not need
some written job analysis to tell them what to do.

"I've also prepared a new form that will help us assess our
employees' performance. It's not related to the job analyses, but
the evaluations are intended to identify those employees who
should be promoted. It really focuses primarily on an employee's
potential. We thought it might be a good idea to standardize
things, because in all honesty we've not emphasized this very much
in the past. To spread the load, we evaluate every white-collar
employee except the top V.P.s once a year during their birth
month. I'm the one who performs these evaluations, so I wanted
to be certain they don't accumulate all at once. This way I have
about ten a month. There's really little need to bother to evaluate the blue-collar employees. I've brought along a copy of the
form we use for each employee evaluated." (This form is shown
as Exhibit 81-2.)

Exhibit 81-2

WORK PERFORMANCE EVALUATION

Rated employee:_____

Salary:_____

Position:_____

I. Work habits

  a. How often is this employee late to work?

1	2	3	4	5	6
less than once/week					more than once/week

  b. How hard does this employee work?

1	2	3	4	5	6
extremely					not very

  c. How frequently does this employee take extended lunch hours?

1	2	3	4	5	6
more than once/week					less than once/week

  d. How frequently does this employee work late?

1	2	3	4	5	6
less than once/week					more than once/week

II. Personal characteristics

  a. How intelligent is this employee?

1	2	3	4	5	6
very					not very

  b. How popular is this employee?

1	2	3	4	5	6
not very					very

  c. How would you rate this employee's personal appearance?

1	2	3	4	5	6
excellent					poor

  d. How often do you trust this employee?

1	2	3	4	5	6
always					never

III. Interpersonal relations

  a. How well does this employee get along with:

	1	2	3	4	5	6
Superiors	1	2	3	4	5	6
Peers	1	2	3	4	5	6
Subordinates	1	2	3	4	5	6
Outsiders	1	2	3	4	5	6
	not well					very well

Exhibit 81-2 (continued)

IV. Supervision

    a. How much supervision does this person need?

1	2	3	4	5	6
a lot					a little

    b. What 3 descriptive words would describe this employee's personality:

        1. _____

        2. _____

        3. _____

    c. How well does this employee accept supervision?

1	2	3	4	5	6
very well					not well

V. General: In 50 words or less, describe this employee's potential for promotion.

VI. Promote:

    Yes _____

    No _____

"I also get involved a bit in career development and employee training. We have given some thought to career planning for our white-collar employees, because its something that benefits VMC as well as the individual employee. We have a career development program where once a year an employee and his or her second-line supervisor get together to assess the employee's strengths and weaknesses. We also discuss the employee's goals and where they would like to go in the company in the future. Both the second-line supervisor and the employee next look at how these individual goals mesh with the needs of VMC in order to develop some realistic plans and strategies the employee can put into effect in order to realize future goals. Although it's difficult to measure the success of the program in real dollar terms, I feel it has been worth the effort. I think we have a responsibility as the senior management at Vanzo to understand each employee's career stage, because you just don't treat a brand new manager the same way you do someone who's been with the firm for 25 years and is in his or her mid-fifties. The issues in their lives are fundamentally different.

"On occasion we'll conduct an employee training program, and if I do say so myself, they have been extremely successful. Let me give you an example. About four months ago, Ms. Vanzo was walking through the plant and observed one of our 14 fork-lift operators improperly loading several pallets. This could have been dangerous, and it could have seriously damaged some of our merchandise. When she discussed this with me, I immediately saw the importance of the problem and got to work on designing a comprehensive employee training program. I assembled all of the fork-lift operators and all the employees who operated any moving vehicles at VMC (approximately 160 employees in all) and put them through a four-and-one-half-day training program. I think they all really got a lot out of the training, because neither Ms. Vanzo nor I have recently seen any problems with the fork lifts.

"As I mentioned, we don't really have much need to develop our 96 management employees, because they all know their jobs fairly well. Its virtually impossible to teach management anyway. Every once in a while, we conduct some role playing, management games, and the like for all management employees. I'm not sure it accomplishes anything, but everyone really seems to enjoy the management development activities and feel good about the process. I also considered trying an assessment center, but I think that's just too sophisticated for us. You're either born a manager or you're not, so there's not much we can do at VMC with our 13 pro-jected new management hires. We should first give them some orientation and then let them learn on the job. Next, let me introduce the third member of our staff, Mr. Harold Thomas, who's responsible for our personnel selection activities at Vanzo."

"Unlike Bill, I know my area of the company is critically important. Others on the staff may do the recruiting, but my job is selection of the best possible employees. As Milt indicated earlier, we've had some turnover problems recently, and I'm really baffled. I wonder, contrary to Bill's comments, if an assessment center could help us solve some of our problems.

Perhaps we could buy a prepackaged one I remember from school.
It dealt with the allocation of scholarship funds. I don't know
what, if anything, we've been doing wrong. We have a six-page
application blank that covers everything we would ever want to
know about a potential employee: age, sex, marital status, children, education, military service, etc. Our policy is that you can
never have too much information about potential employees. We
conduct a personality inventory and a polygraph test for each
new employee just to be certain we know who we're considering. I
personally screen each of the application blanks, and I sit down
and place all potential employees in a rank order based upon my
subjective assessment of the contribution each individual can make
to Vanzo Manufacturing. Then as soon as a position opens up, we
offer the person a job. I for one would certainly be interested in
any thoughts our new college graduate would have. Let me turn
things over to Ray Anderson, our V.P. of Manufacturing."

Mr. Anderson begins by saying, "Ms. Vanzo, there are several
things that require immediate attention. First of all, we need
employee training desperately. This bunk about fork-lift training
is just that--bunk. I've been complaining about our training, or
lack of it, for 12 months. One of my new employees is going to
set up the training I want. Our absenteeism and turnover certainly
would be lower if the union wasn't always complaining about their
work rules. I want our new contract to state that management can
do whatever is necessary so we can meet our production goals. I
would also like to strongly disagree with the notion of S. Comfort
reporting to you, Ms. Vanzo, rather than me. All manufacturing
should report to me, and I don't like this proposed organization.

"Another major problem is manufacturing's getting three new
management hires when we are expected to increase production by
approximately 70 percent. This is untenable. I've said enough.
Roger, it's your turn."

Roger Hartell, the marketing V.P., begins by saying, "I
agree with most of Ray's comments. One new hire is not anywhere
near the number of people I need to insure success of the fiscal
year 82-83 sales plan. Personnel gets nine new employees, and
manufacturing and marketing get four. Someone must be empire
building. I also want to mention the lack of benefits for my
salespeople. I've lost several good salespeople in the past six
months due to our lack of competitive benefits. We do not have a
competitive bonus plan or acceptable gas mileage allowances, tire
allowances or meal payment plans that our competitors have.
Things have gotten worse since we brought some large distributors
on board. Our benefits are worse than most of our large distributors'. We will never reach our sales target for fiscal year 82-83
unless we do something now. I don't care about other employees;
we've got to take care of our good salespeople. That's where
we make our money. O.K., Mike, I've said enough; it's your
turn in the barrel."

Mike Klubier, the V.P. of quality assurance, rises and begins
speaking. "I flatly assert that we will not reach our sales goal
unless I get 10 more people immediately! Our product is suspect

on quality as it is right now. How are we going to ship 70 percent more product with the same quality assurance staff? We will have nothing but diminished quality. I know that the upcoming contract negotiations and the southern plan situation will also make my department's job more challenging. I recommend, Ms. Vanzo, that you reconsider hiring those nine people in personnel and reallocate those positions to me. Personnel, manufacturing and marketing may need people, but I need them more!"

"Well its been a long, but hopefully productive afternoon," says Ms. Vanzo. "I appreciate the preparation and candor from each of you. I'm sure there are others who have relevant issues to discuss, but we should probably call it a day. I think this will be invaluable to contributing to a "fresh eye" analysis of the personnel management policies and procedures of the Vanzo Manufacturing Company. As part of the VMC family now, you're of course free to spend some time wandering around the plant with your eyes and ears open. We'll all be anxiously awaiting your analysis."

As any good assistant to the president, you want to spend some additional time observing firsthand the operations at VMC. Here are some of the situations you observe.

As you leave the conference room and head toward the plant floor, you are stopped by an obviously bewildered individual who introduces himself as Sam Wilhelmi, a new employee. He asks for directions to the personnel office; he says he is late for his initial orientation. You decide to accompany Mr. Wilhelmi to the personnel office to observe what takes place. Sam takes a seat in the office and then waits for about an hour until six new employees arrive. Mr. Wilkie, a VMC employee, welcomes them to the company and then the "paper blitz" takes place. In the next 30 minutes, he gives them a lot of paper--work rules, benefits, pay forms to fill out, and so on. It appears as though Sam's head is swimming. Then Sam gets a slip telling him to report to his new supervisor, Andrew Wilkerson, in Room 810. Andrew takes him around the facility for three minutes and then points out Sam's new workbench and wishes him good luck.

While in the personnel office, you pick up some of the literature provided to new employees. One brochure is titled "Benefits and Services Available to VMC Employees." As you scan through the pamphlet, you see the following list of available benefits and services:

1. Unemployment compensation
2. 14 days paid vacation
3. One sick day/month
4. Free medical care for the VMC employee; 50 percent of medical costs paid by VMC for the family of VMC employees up to a ceiling of $1500 per year
5. Social Security
6. Free dental care
7. 6 paid holidays per year
8. Cafeteria privileges

As you again head for the plant floor, you run into Mr. Samuel Johnson, the chief union steward whom Ms. Vanzo mentioned earlier in the day. He sees the booklet in your hand and remarks that the booklet will have to be three times as thick after the contract negotiations in a few months. Mr. Johnson remarks, "Old Ms. Vanzo never asks us what benefits we want. This was one of the big factors in favor of our union. Now we have a voice. Plus the whole benefits package is messed up; our wages are often docked during our supposedly "paid" vacations and holidays, and our spouses' medical bills take months to be reimbursed. We also do not like the new southern plant situation at all. We hear you're going to lay off the rest of us and move everything there. That's one thing you better not try!" Although you are sure Mr. Johnson could go on, you decide it is best to end this conversation.

Unfortunately Mr. Johnson is reluctant for you to leave. He seems determined to send a message to Ms. Vanzo. Mr. Johnson continues, "As far as I'm concerned we may have reached an impasse with management. Its ironic; we haven't even begun negotiating and we're at an impasse. That's typical of management's attitude, though. I'm not sure whether we ought to seek mediation or arbitration or what--maybe we should even consider a strike--but I'll tell you the situation is pretty bad. We have a fairly substantial strike fund accumulated, and I also think we expect some support from the national. I'm not sure the company's inventories are in very great shape though. This may be to our advantage. If talks break down, as I suspect they will, I plan to invite Mr. Herman Cherish in to serve as a mediator as long as he's acceptable to management. He's been a member of the F.M.C.S. for 11 years and is widely respected as a mediator who specializes in working within the manufacturing industry. I think we will need the most experienced mediator we can find, because I expect some trouble."

You realize that it would be desirable to spend more time observing, but you had best get to work on your analysis. It looks like this challenge may have been even greater than you had anticipated.

As you get into your car, you think about how easy things were back in school. Now it's time to get to work analyzing the personnel management policies and procedures of the Vanzo Manufacturing Company.

TEACHING COMMENTARY

This case was developed by Major Jeffrey A. McNally, who co-authored Case 1, "Pacific Aircraft Company." Many of the personnel/human resources issues apparent in the "Pacific Aircraft Company" case are very similar to those in the "Vanzo Manufacturing Company" case. Major McNally has used the VMC case primarily as an examination case, and we agree that the variety of personnel/ human resources issues presented makes it an excellent candidate to use as a capstone or examination case.

For general purposes of case analysis, reference should be made to the commentaries and suggested plans of action suggested for the "Pacific Aircraft Company" case on pages 21 to 26 of this Instructor's Manual. Other key issues, in addition to those high- lighted in the PAC case, are as follows.

1. Focus on the adversarial nature of the relations between the union and management; the differences in perceptions regarding relations as expressed by the vice president of personnel and the chief union steward; the company's treatment of overtime wages and the law as defined under the Fair Labor Standards Act; the leverage each side presents on the contractual issues mentioned (job security, automation, work rules, etc.); the company's proposed tactics during the authorization card- signing drive in its southern plant; and the possibility of National Labor Relations Board (NLRB) intervention.

2. In addition to EEOC regulations, the company is faced with OSHA guidelines; discuss the company's attitude towards those regulations. In this regard, discuss how management can inadvertently but actively "promote" a union through its positions on various issues. Identify other areas in the case where this may be happening.

3. The VMC case provides insights into the interdependencies be- tween departments with a company. Identify the differences in priorities discussed by the representatives of each department; how these individuals demonstrate fairly insular interests rather than planning for the future of the company as a whole; and the problems the company faces in trying to allocate scarce resources (in this situation, new hires) to meet their best uses and objectives.

4. This case presents an excellent opportunity to discuss the importance of performance evaluation--i.e., who should be evaluated, how often, what type of assessment form to use, the need to tie performance evaluation back to the job requirements as specified through job analysis, etc. Students should be able to present fairly thorough critiques of the performance evaluation form presented by Bill Donalds.

5. Discuss the importance of incentives for improving productivity, efficiency, and competitive positioning. Solicit suggestions for incentive plans that cover production employees (keeping

in mind the importance of product quality) and plans for the sales personnel.

6. Critique the benefits and services list presented to new employees in the orientation material. Discussion should focus on the presentation of the benefits and services and the degree of specificity provided for each item.

CASE 82

THE BYPASSED SUPERVISOR

Until this year Jim Floyd had been happy working for Fitzgerald Conveyor Corporation. Jim had started eight years ago in Fitzgerald's new assembly plant as a lab technician, and within one year he was promoted into an engineering job. As an engineer, he acted as liaison between corporate engineering and the plant production departments in introducing and explaining changes required in current production. Another of Jim's major responsibilities was to seek ways to correct defective parts and subassembly secions so that they could be salvaged and used in production. He was also heavily involved in yearly model changes and provided corporate engineering with feedback on tooling and production problems in the assembly of the new conveyors. The engineering department manager, Helen Green, relied on Jim's problem-solving expertise. She frequently complimented Jim on his performance and passed along numerous favorable comments she received on Jim's efficiency from other department managers.

Jim was one of six engineers in the department, all of whom reported directly to department manager Green. Approximately two years ago, however, a new position of engineering supervisor was created to lighten the burden of the department manager. The engineering supervisor's principal responsibility was to assist in supervising the engineers, and the individual reported directly to the department manager. Bob Butler, one of the older engineers who had worked with Jim Floyd, was promoted to this new position. Butler had started with the Fitzgerald Corporation in the corporate engineering offices and had transferred to the new assembly plant when it was built. Butler was a specialist in electrical circuitry, having limited knowledge of most of the mechanical engineering, tooling, and production aspects of the plant. Further, Butler had no previous supervisory training or experience, but he felt that he would have no trouble supervising the engineers in the department. Butler felt that the engineers were very knowledgeable in their individual areas of responsibility and a pretty independent group as well. Because of this, Bob decided that if he tended to leave the engineers alone to handle their own areas of responsibility, he would have few problems.

Jim Floyd did not greet Butler's promotion with enthusiasm since he felt Bob Butler's performance as an engineer and his

_____

All names are disguised.

limited knowledge of the other engineers' responsibilities did
not warrant this promotion. Nevertheless, Jim decided to make
the best of the situation and to perform in the same manner for
Butler as he had when he reported directly to department manager
Green.

However, because of his general lack of knowledge in various
areas of plant operations, Butler could not make decisions necessary to give proper direction to Jim and the other engineers so
they could perform their jobs satisfactorily. Soon Jim Floyd
and the other engineers simply bypassed Bob and returned to contacting department manager Green directly for information and
needed decisions; this allowed them to operate more efficiently.
Seemingly, Green approved of this procedure since she bypassed
Bob Butler on several occasions, too. This confirmed Jim's feeling
of Butler's inadequacy as a supervisor.

Everything was fine until six months later when Green was
promoted to a new job, and Ellwood Roth was brought in as the new
department manager. Mr. Roth had been an engineering supervisor
for many years at one of the older plants in the corporation, and
he and Bob Butler had become good friends over the years.

After Mr. Roth took over as department manager, the engineers
began and continued to go directly to him for information and
decisions concerning their areas of responsibility, again bypassing
Bob Butler, who had resented the practice ever since it had started.
Butler had not had much chance to change this practice before. But
with his old friend Mr. Roth as the new department manager, Butler
complained to him about being bypassed and having no control over
the engineers--especially Jim Floyd. Mr. Roth immediately informed
all the engineers, individually, that Bob Butler was their immediate supervisor and that all questions and information should
go through Butler, who also was to give them their work assignments. Jim Floyd greeted this announcement with even less enthusiasm, since by this time he had little respect for Bob Butler
and no confidence in his ability to direct the work of the engineers.

Mr. Roth soon found, however, that he could get quicker and
more accurate information and action by going directly to the
engineer responsible for a particular area, thus bypassing Butler.
He began doing so on things he considered urgent. The engineers
had been going to Butler with questions and information as they
were instructed, but after Mr. Roth had given them assignments or
questioned them directly on plant problems several times, they
again began contacting Roth directly.

Bob Butler became increasingly upset when the engineers began
bypassing him again. In Butler's mind, Jim Floyd was primarily
responsible for the situation since Jim seldom talked to him and
would not discuss anything other than work. Butler did not care
too much for Jim personally, and since he felt Jim was turning the
other engineers against him, he decided to blame Jim for the by-
passing situation. Butler complained of this to Roth by telling
him, "Jim Floyd has a poor attitude. Floyd does not respect me,

and he is the man who single-handedly has tried to turn the other engineers against me!"

With this complaint from Bob Butler, Mr. Roth called both Bob and Jim into his office. Mr. Roth told Jim about Bob's charges and said that either he "settle any differences with Bob and shape up" or he would take "drastic action." He also told Jim again that Bob was his boss, and all information and decisions needed were to be directed to him.

This made Jim Floyd very angry and upset because he felt that he had been doing his job properly and performing satisfactorily. Maybe, he thought, Butler was deliberately or otherwise distorting the information given to Mr. Roth. Consequently, Jim started writing everything he gave to Butler. Whenever Mr. Roth asked him directly for information, Jim would write the information and give it to Bob Butler to forward to Mr. Roth.

A few weeks later Bob Butler called Jim Floyd into his office. Butler was visibly angry when he told Jim that he was disgusted with him for not talking to him except to answer a direct question. Butler told Floyd, "If you don't shape up and do better work, I will discharge you, and it will be good riddance!"

As he returned to his desk, Jim Floyd wondered what he should do.

THE BYPASSED SUPERVISOR

TEACHING COMMENTARY

The following analysis of this case was developed by a graduate student at Washington University as a written assignment included in a graduate course in human resources management.

This case is a prime example of a violation of the principle of unity of command on the part of two department managers and the problems it can cause. The original department manager, Helen Green, evidently had difficulty in giving control of the engineers to the new supervisor, Mr. Butler. By continuing to go directly to the engineers, Green undermined the supervisor at a very critical period. The first few months a new supervisory position is in existence are crucial in establishing the duties and responsibilities of that position. I feel the original department manager (Green) should have made sure that she issued directions and requests through the new supervisor. Green should also have told the engineers to ask their supervisor (Butler) before they came to her with questions. If the engineers told her they had already talked to the supervisor, and he couldn't give them the answer, Green should have talked with Butler to see what was needed to provide him with the answers he needed.

When Mr. Roth became department manager, I feel there was no excuse for him to bypass his supervisor, Butler, or condone such action by the engineers. If the position had been properly established before Mr. Roth took over the department, he may not have started bypassing the supervisor; but since it had not been properly established, Roth should have done the job himself. Apparently Mr. Butler was not a strong individual, but if either of the department managers were aware of this fact, they did nothing to correct the situation.

I also question the original department manager's wisdom in choosing Bob Butler to fill the new supervisor's position. Butler provides an example of what can happen when a supervisor is chosen from within a department. Making a person engineering supervisor just because he is the "best engineer" or has been with the company longest is not necessarily a good choice. In this case, the person chosen to be the new supervisor was far from being the best engineer in the department! While it is not known what the other engineers thought of Butler as an engineer, Jim Floyd's feelings about Bob Butler's performance as an engineer and lack of knowledge of the other engineers' areas of responsibility indicate that Butler may not have been too highly regarded by the other engineers, either. If this were the case, he probably would not have been too effective, even with full backing by both department managers. Butler's lack of supervisory training or experience was no doubt a large part of the cause of his troubles with Jim Floyd and the other engineers. With training or experience, Butler may have handled the situation with Floyd differently and probably would not have let personalities or personal feelings influence his actions. Because of the poor beginning in the new supervisory position and lack of support from either of the department managers, I doubt if Bob Butler will ever be effective as engineering supervisor in that department as long as the original engineers are still there.

THE BYPASSED SUPERVISOR

Jim Floyd is an example of what can happen to an employee's attitude and morale. The change in reporting to a supervisor instead of the department manager may have made Jim feel that he was losing status. Violation of the principle of unity of command by both department managers made matters even worse. Floyd's reaction appears to have been a decrease in work output and resentment of his new supervisor for not taking some action to correct the situation. Jim's lack of respect for his supervisor evidently showed and caused Bob Butler to let personalities and personal feelings influence his actions. I feel that Jim probably could have tried to react differently, possibly by trying even harder to do a good job or at least maintain the same work output as before. He also might have tried talking to Bob Butler more as a possible way of avoiding conflict with him.

DISCUSSION QUESTIONS

1. Why did Helen Green choose to permit the engineers to bypass Bob Butler? Why did the new department manager, Mr. Roth, continue this practice?
2. Analyze Bob Butler's supervisory approach from being a "laissez faire" supervisor at first to becoming an "autocratic" supervisor at the latter stages of the case.
3. What should Jim Floyd do at the end of this case? Consider the alternatives open to him.

CASE 83

THE COLLEGE PROTESTER

Jane Washington, a student at Hill City Junior College, was
nineteen years old and in the second semester of her freshman year
at the time of this case. To support herself while attending
college, Jane had accepted employment with Sanders Supermarket
Store, a unit of a major chain of food stores in Hill City.

The store in which Jane worked as a check-out clerk is located
in a predominantly white community, populated primarily by blue-
collar (or working-class) families. Jane worked approximately
fifteen to twenty hours a week, during evenings and on weekends
as she was available and needed. Her performance had been rated
as satisfactory by her supervisors during her six months of employment.

CAMPUS UNREST

In early 1970 a series of events at Hill City Junior College
led to a serious situation of student unrest on the campus. On
one occasion dissident students occupied several buildings, and
frequent protest demonstrations by black students culminated in
a severe demonstration protesting the Vietnam War. The partial
burning of a building during this demonstration led to the closing
of the campus for several days. Jane Washington became interested
in campus problems, and she was quite sympathetic with the student
protests and issues that had been raised. Following a major student demonstration involving antiwar sentiments and protesting the
killing of several students on other campuses in the United States,
Jane Washington could contain herself no longer. She decided that
she had to make known her feelings to everyone, including people
with whom she came in contact on her job at Sanders Supermarket.

Jane reported for work on a Saturday morning at the supermarket
with a black band around her left arm clearly displayed over the
neat uniform that had been furnished by the store. In addition,
several large buttons were attached to her uniform that protested
the Vietnam War and discrimination against blacks. Her supervisor,
Helen Dulo, noticed these items, but she said nothing to Jane
because she did not know what action would be appropriate.

All names and places are disguised.

216

CUSTOMER PROTESTS

Within several hours after Jane Washington had come to work, numerous customers whose groceries had been checked by her had commented on the armband and the protest buttons. Several went directly to the store manager, George Jamieson, to complain. These customers said they thought it was very inappropriate for a college student to express herself politically in a store that was supposed to be neutral on political matters. Mr. Jamieson, after hearing several of the customers' complaints, agreed with them. He told Miss Dulo to tell Miss Washington to remove the buttons and the protest armband.

THE ULTIMATUM

At 11:45 a.m., about fifteen minutes before Jane was to go to lunch, Miss Dulo asked her to come to her office for a conference. The general nature of the conversation between Miss Dulo and Jane Washington was as follows:

> Miss Dulo: We have received several complaints about your protest buttons and the black armband. We do not care what you do or what you say off the job, but while you are at work here in our store, you must remove these armbands and buttons and wear only the authorized uniform.

> Jane Washington: And if I choose to do otherwise?

> Miss Dulo: If you choose to do otherwise, we will have no recourse but to suspend or discharge you since we need to maintain the confidence of the customers we have in this community. We will give you a little time to think about it, but before you report back to work next Monday, you'd better make up your mind. We hope you will come to work as usual without the band and buttons.

THE NEWSPAPER STORY

That afternoon Jane Washington went to Mr. Jamieson's office and told him that she was resigning from her position at the supermarket because she could not, in good conscience, work at a store where she was denied freedom of speech. After telling Mr. Jamieson this, she went to her home, where she called a local newspaper reporter to relate the situation as it had occurred. She told the reporter that she had been fired because she was not permitted to exercise her individual freedom of expression while an employee at the supermarket. The newspaper reporter contacted the supermarket manager, Mr. Jamieson, and asked for his version of the story. Mr. Jamieson replied that the company had to protect its business. He stated that no employee while in the store was allowed to wear unauthorized clothing or buttons that openly expressed opinions about controversial political or social issues.

217

The next day the story was a front-page item in the local newspaper. On the following Monday morning many students at Hill City Junior College were irate because of the supermarket's treatment of Jane Washington. They suggested a boycott of the Sanders chain, and they organized a brief afternoon protest demonstration outside the store. A number of store employees--particularly part-time students working in the supermarket--joined in the protest demonstration, and several employees and numerous citizens wrote letters of protest to the management.

Several days after the protest demonstration and the publicity in the newspaper, Mr. Jamieson called a meeting of supervisors in his store as well as supervisors from several other Sanders Supermarkets located in Hill City. He opened the meeting by raising several major questions for consideration by the management: "Should we rescind our actions in the Jane Washington situation? Second, what policies do we need in order to cope with future situations of this sort? Further, should we change our policies or rules on employee dress, behavior, and appearance, and if so, how should these be developed?"

THE COLLEGE PROTESTOR

TEACHING COMMENTARY

This is a type of case situation that is not unfamiliar to many companies and their managers. Although it occurred during the Vietnam War era, the case is illustrative of a broader cultural problem in American society: namely, at what point does an individual's right of self-expression as a free citizen come into conflict with his or her relationship and obligation to an employer?

Many young people believe strongly that the individual's right to protest is sacred in America and that it is the duty of organizations to take positions on controversial political and social issues. Yet most managers believe that their organizations generally must remain neutral on public issues, particularly on ones where customer opinion is extremely divided.

DISCUSSION QUESTIONS

1. Was Mr. Jamieson, the manager of the supermarket, justified in ordering Jane Washington to remove protest buttons and the armband from her work uniform?
2. Evaluate Jane Washington's claim that she was denied "freedom of speech."
3. Are there limits to the exercise of freedom of expression in the employee-employer relationship? Why is a newspaper story on this type of issue of serious concern to the management of the store?
4. At the end of the case, outline a series of recommendations for Mr. Jamieson in response to the questions that he posed at his meeting of supervisors.
5. Develop a policy statement for Sanders Supermarkets that could govern future issues of employee dress, appearance, and so on.

CASE 84

TARDY TOO OFTEN

Henry Howell, commissioner of the State Department for Legal Assistance, took office on September 1, 1983. He soon became aware that he had a tardiness problem among his staff. On December 15 he issued the following memorandum:

> It is the responsibility of every staff member to be on the job at 8:00 a.m. However, only those staff members who come in after 8:30 a.m. will be considered late.

The tardiness problem continued and on March 21, 1984, Mr. Howell issued a second memorandum:

> The work day for this department is from 8:00 a.m. to 4:30 p.m., Monday through Friday, unless otherwise specified. All staff persons must sign attendance sheets at the receptionist's desk.

The tardiness situation did not improve. In fact, it became worse with the advent of snow, ice, and falling temperatures during the months of November and December. The second memorandum was followed on January 3, 1985, with still a third:

> Effective Monday, January 7, all employees must adhere to the 8:00 a.m. starting time. Failure to comply with the 8:00 a.m. starting time will result in immediate suspension. The only accepted deviation from this policy will be on days of inclement weather such as the previous few days, when the temperature dropped to 15-20 degrees below zero in the morning.

Robert Perkins reported to work at 8:30 a.m. on January 8, 1985. Deputy Commissioner George Tomkin immediately suspended Perkins without pay for that day for violating the January 3 memorandum. On January 10, Perkins sent Tomkin the following letter:

> I feel that the excuse I gave when I called in at 7:58 a.m., notifying the receptionist that I would be a few minutes late due to the fact that

All names are disguised.

> I had certain marital obligations that I had
> no other alternative but to deal with was a
> valid excuse and would be handled with con-
> sideration.
>   I feel the suspension was illegal and I will
> seek any means necessary to recover the eight
> hours of wages lost due to this suspension.

George Tomkin was surprised at Perkins's strong reply, feeling that
the penalty was very reasonable under all the circumstances. He
immediately arranged a meeting.

Tomkin reviewed Perkins's record with him. The record indicated
that he had been late for work on several occasions during the
two-week pay period December 26, 1984-January 8, 1985. During
these two weeks he was late 142 minutes, using 8:00 a.m. as the
basis for making the computation. For the 10 weeks (five pay
periods) ending January 8, 1985, his tardiness totalled 472 minutes,
although some of the lost minutes were due to inclement weather.

In addition, the record showed that Perkins, as Tomkin termed it,
had "falsified" his reporting-in time on several occasions. In
order to keep an accurate record of tardiness among the staff,
Tomkin had a staff receptionist maintain a secret log of the actual
reporting-in time of all personnel. This record was periodically
checked against the reporting-in time each employee recorded on
the regular log. The records indicated that on occasion Perkins
had entered an earlier reporting-in time than the time entered by
the receptionist on the secret log.

Perkins felt that he had not been suspended for good reason, but
that the State Department for Legal Assistance had acted in an
"arbitrary and capricious manner" in suspending him. He reminded
Tomkin that the workday policy was as stated in the commissioner's
memorandum of December 15, 1983; that is, the normal starting
time was 8:00 a.m. with a 30-minute grace period. The policy, as
stated in that memorandum, was consistent with both past and
present practices. The March 21 memorandum, according to Perkins,
did not alter the existing policy or practice.

Perkins informed Tomkin that he had checked the policy with several
other employees who also interpreted current policy to allow the
30-minute grace period. These employees would be willing to
testify to that effect, if asked.

Perkins pointed out that almost all employees, at one time or
another, entered an earlier reporting-in time than was actually
the case. This occurred most frequently during the winter months
when staff members would run up to the office, sign in, and then
go back out to park their car. He suggested that the receptionist
might well have recorded the second arrival of employees, since
she was frequently called away from her desk to run errands to
other parts of the building.

In reviewing the record with Tomkin, Perkins pointed out that
three employees, in addition to himself, had signed in after

8:00 a.m. on January 7, and none of them had been suspended. Furthermore, on January 8 three employees, including Perkins, signed in after 8:00 a.m. However, he was the only one of the three who was suspended; he was also the only one of the three who had called in to alert the receptionist that he would be late or who had supplied her in advance with the reason for reporting in after 8:00 a.m.

George Tomkin closed the meeting with Robert Perkins with a promise that he would give Perkins a decision in two days. Tomkin was aware that Perkins could file a formal grievance under the state's employment policy procedures, if he should decide to stay with his original decision to suspend Perkins for one day. Tomkin wondered whether he should consult his boss, Mr. Howell, for help in this matter.

TEACHING COMMENTARY

This case can be used to illustrate a number of problem areas that are quite common in the practice of personnel/human resources management. Among these are the following: (a) the problem of excessive employee tardiness; (b) the need for clearly communicated and consistent policies in regard to attendance and tardiness; (c) administration of discipline; (d) how employees are likely to challenge what they consider to be unfair or inconsistent treatment.

DISCUSSION QUESTIONS

1. Did the memorandum of January 3, 1985, change the department's policy?
2. Had Perkins been given adequate warning before being suspended?
3. Should Perkins's tardiness record before January 7 have been considered in deciding to suspend him? Should reporting in after 8:00 a.m. but before 8:30 a.m. be considered tardy under the policy existing before January 7?
4. How do you evaluate Perkins's statement that on occasion almost all employees at one time or another would enter on the log a reporting-in time earlier than their actual starting time?
5. How do you evaluate the failure of the department to take disciplinary action against other tardy employees?
6. If you were George Tomkin, what would you do now?
7. How do you believe an impartial arbitrator would rule on this case?